Astrolographs

JULIA TOPAZ

Illustrations by
Giacomo Bagnara

CHRONICLE BOOKS
SAN FRANCISCO

Astrolo

graphs

How the Zodiac Signs Behave (AND MISBEHAVE) in Love, Work, Leisure, and Beyond, IN 112 HUMOROUS CHARTS

Library of Congress Cataloging-in-Publication Data available.

ISBN 978-1-7972-3137-2

Manufactured in China.

Illustrations by Giacomo Bagnara.
Design by Rachel Harrell.

10 9 8 7 6 5 4 3 2 1

Chronicle books and gifts are available at special quantity discounts to corporations, professional associations, literacy programs, and other organizations. For details and discount information, please contact our premiums department at corporatesales@chroniclebooks.com or at 1-800-759-0190.

Chronicle Books LLC
680 Second Street
San Francisco, California 94107
www.chroniclebooks.com

CONTENTS

CHAPTER 1

The Zodiac Signs Do Everyday Life

CHAPTER 2

The Zodiac Signs Do Fun & Leisure

CHAPTER 3

The Zodiac Signs Do Love

THE LANGUAGE OF ASTROLOGY

Astrology is a language, an art, and a method for answering existential questions through a spiritual and observational lens. I like to think of it as people-watching combined with philosophy. And once you fully embrace it, it becomes a lens through which you look at everything.

Astrology, once learned, becomes like breathing: You can stop thinking about it, but you can't stop doing it!

I've been studying astrology for more than a decade, and one of my favorite things to do is to guess someone's zodiac sign when I'm first getting to know them. I was once on a date with a guy who kept responding no to every request I made. It was odd; he would later change his mind and be collaborative, but his immediate reaction was always to begin with no. After a few rounds of this, I said, "You must be a Taurus!" He indeed was a Taurus, and he was pretty stunned that I was able to guess his sign.

Because I understand astrology, I can quickly see what's behind a person's behavior and whims. In the case of my date, I recognized the core energy of the Taurus archetype. Taurus's entire essence is safety, predictability, comfort, and accumulating and retaining resources. Saying "no" is the instinctive way we have to keep ourselves safe. Saying "no" is a boundary, a line in the sand; we reclaim our right to sovereignty and agency. And once we've claimed the right to refuse, we can actually begin to open up from this place of safety. That's just one example of why Taurus can be so hell-bent on their no, while other zodiac signs don't really feel the need for that, as safety isn't such a preoccupation or drive.

After many years studying the astrology language and observing people (one really can't exist without the other), I started to feel an almost evangelical zeal to convert as many people as I could—a kind of astrology crusade, if you will. In everything I did as an astrologer, I always had the same goal: I wanted to reach as many people as possible and share what I consider to be an incredible cave of wonders.

As I thought about how to reach as many people as possible, I realized there was an opportunity to share astrology in a new way.

In general, there are two types of astrology content: deeply interesting, detailed, dense literature only people already well-versed in astrology would read. This type of content is great—and personally I devour these books—but it's also incredibly niche and you must have prerequisites. You can't just go from "I'm a Scorpio" to "Let's read about the aspects between my Moon and Saturn and how it makes me fearful to be vulnerable." There are so many steps before you can be initiated to such depth.

The other common type of astrology content is general horoscopes. These can be entertaining but they are often devoid of any substance. Everyone can enjoy reading them every now and then, but no one truly puts their faith into it and for good reason—they're incredibly generalist.

I quickly understood that if I wanted people to be interested in discovering my astrological cave of wonders, I had to aim for a very precise balance: horoscope-type content (fun, lighthearted, easy to consume) but also oddly specific. The kind of substance that you recognize and pulls you in to dig deeper. It's obviously not easy to do; there's a reason why things were either one or the other; the balance of the two is truly finicky work—but trust a gal with four planets in Libra to attempt the impossible: perfect balance!

I saw an opportunity to focus on the essence behind each zodiac sign and find very specific manifestations of their true nature. Everyone knows the stereotype of Cancers being emotional and indirect, but when you call them out for posting elusive Instagram captions in the hope of catching their ex's interest, it's an unexpected callout, one that might make them pause for a second and self-reflect.

Once I began to see the world this way, I couldn't stop. I'd observe people around me and notice things that are totally trivial and yet so unique. I'd see my Virgo friend hoarding napkins as if they were an essential item for their survival. Open the glove compartment in their car and find yourself swarmed by them "just in case, you never know!" I'd see my Leo friends wearing such colorful clothing (who else buys yellow outfits, truly?).

And though I don't believe the archetypes of our Sun sign form our whole personality, I do believe there are only twelve types of energies, which we all display with varying degrees and varying priority.

In this book, I reveal the essence behind each zodiac sign's energy, capturing the nature of each sign through seemingly trivial behaviors. Whether you are a novice or an astrology whiz, I'll invite you to explore at your comfort level and provide you with tools to take a deeper look at astrology and yourself.

My unwavering passion is sharing the magic and wonder of astrology with as many folks as possible. I hope this lighthearted, fun, and sassy take—rooted in deep knowledge—helps you understand new things about yourself, your relationships, and the world.

Getting Started

Within this book, you'll discover fun-to-read visuals—graphs, charts, timelines, and more—carefully crafted to unveil the unique traits, inclinations, and proclivities that each zodiac sign embodies. The book is organized into three chapters, with information on how the signs handle everyday life, fun and leisure, and love and relationships.

Your natural inclination will likely be to dive headfirst into the information associated with your Sun sign. Of course the Sun is used to getting all the attention and spotlight—everything revolves around it, right? You can absolutely refer to your Sun sign to read the graphs; however, within each chapter, I will offer a deeper way of looking at astrology, yourself, and this book. Every section includes illuminating information to help you look beyond your Sun sign to see how other aspects of your birth chart impact your behavior in each area of your life.

And while your own graphs might be your initial go-to, you'll soon begin envisioning others in your life. Your partner, your parents, your closest friends, or even that one colleague you don't exactly see eye to eye with will all spring to mind. It's the beauty of astrology—it offers insight not just into your own cosmic makeup but also into those around you, fostering more empathy, love, and connection.

Read on to find tools to help you get started on your astrological journey, if your curiosity leads you to seeking a deeper read than your Sun sign.

BIRTH CHART 101

To truly understand a person through the astrological lens, we delve into their *birth chart*. The birth chart takes into account the positions of all the planets at the time and location of a person's birth. This means that even though you might be an Aries Sun, you could have four planets happily stationed in comfy Taurus. If that were the case, you might discover an uncanny identification with Taurus-themed, give-me-my-snack entries.

Learning your birth chart is a great exercise for anyone with an interest in astrology, but especially if you are someone who has always felt like you don't fully resonate with your Sun sign and the stereotypes associated with it: This is for you.

The perspective of astrology is that your personality and psyche are represented by your birth chart, which contains ten planets located in twelve zodiac signs. If that sounds complex, I agree! Let's try to decipher it all in simple steps below.

If you're interested in learning more about your birth chart placements, you can pull your birth chart on many websites including mine, at www.lookupthestars.com.

Personal Planets

The birth chart contains ten planets. For the purpose of this book, we are only exploring "personal planets," which are organized on the following page. Personal planets, as the name indicates, are deeply personal and represent various parts of our psyche.

There are four planets we won't be using for the purpose of this book. The "social planets" (Jupiter, Saturn) and "outer planets" (Uranus, Neptune, Pluto) are more indicative of patterns within a generation rather than on an individual level.

ASTROLOGICAL BODY	WHAT IT REPRESENTS	USE IT FOR
SUN ☉	Your identity, confidence, ego, self-esteem, vitality, and narrative around self.	Any section in this book.
MOON ☽	Your emotions, emotional needs, vulnerable self, and intimacy needs.	Sections related to your emotions and your intimate relationships.
MERCURY ☿	Your intellect, how you think, how you communicate, and your mental filters.	Sections connected with thinking and communication.
VENUS ♀	Your pleasures, aesthetic, values, relationship to money, love, and hedonistic activities.	Sections connected with romantic relationships, money, relaxation, and leisure.
MARS ♂	Your drive, anger, desire, approach to conflict, sexuality, masculine side, and professional activity.	Sections related to conflict, passion, and professional activity.

Zodiac Houses

Your birth chart is also composed of twelve houses. Each house represents a different area of your life. For example, the 2nd house represents our income, resources, and possessions. When the Moon—which represents our emotions—is in the 2nd house, we feel very emotionally tied to our money and the security it provides. The 5th house is play, creativity, and personal expression. When Mars is in the 5th house, we're very driven to play, to compete, and be boldly expressive. In this book, we'll mostly refer to planets, but it can be helpful to understand the houses and what they mean as you learn more about your birth chart.

Each zodiac house is associated with a zodiac sign. For example, the 1st house is the house of Aries. The 10th house is the house of Capricorn. When someone has several planets clustered in a zodiac sign in their birth chart, the house in which those planets are located can provide a lot of helpful information. For example, if you have a cluster of planets in Capricorn, you might resonate a lot with the archetype of being hard-working, adult, responsible, and disciplined.

Where the planets appear in the zodiac houses is entirely dependent on your time of birth, so this additional layer of analysis is only available for those who have an accurate time of birth.

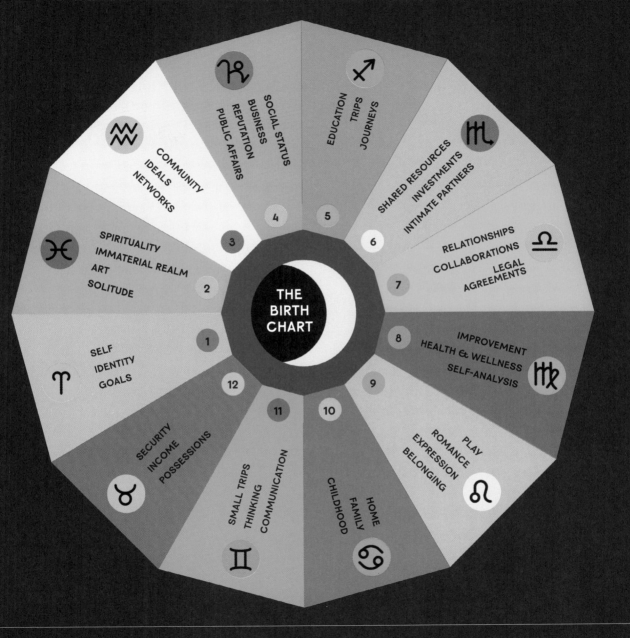

The "Big Three"

In astrology, it's common to hear people reference their "big three," which refers to their Sun, Moon, and rising signs. These three parts of your chart are indeed important and can reveal a lot about your identity, emotions, and how you are perceived by others.

Sun ☉

Sun in the birth chart represents your identity and the narratives you hold around who you are. Sun represents how we identify, the traits we like to embody, and the characteristics we naturally gravitate toward. Sun is the statements we make about ourselves: "I'm bold! I'm confident! I'm an extrovert!" You can see Sun as your personal branding.

Moon ☽

Moon in the birth chart represents who we are on the inside, what we need, how we experience our emotions. If we don't make an effort to tune in, we might not realize our Moon traits, because Moon represents what's happening within. Moon, unlike the Sun, is not something we are particularly conscious of unless we pay attention to our inner world, but Moon represents our emotional needs and our relationship to our emotions, which is arguably quite important. With Sun you might say "I'm confident!" but your Moon might say "I really need words of affirmation. I feel scared when no one looks at me."

Rising ↑

The rising sign, also referred to as ascendant sign, represents how we face the world, what "face" we present, and therefore represents not only how we instinctively interact with the world, but also how other people tend to see us, if they don't look further than their first impression. The rising sign says "This is what I present first when I interact with the world, because instinctively this is my strategy."

1

The Zodiac Signs Do Everyday Life

We'll begin slow and easy by taking a peek at the zodiac signs in their mundane, day-to-day living. We'll start by waking up the zodiac signs! Discover how each sign faces a new day, including who's likely to rise and shine and who's more inclined to snooze the dreaded and nagging alarm.

Next, we'll scrutinize the fundamental needs of each zodiac sign, drawing inspiration from Maslow's hierarchy of needs. We'll take a lighthearted jab at what you truly need to become your best and most powerful self!

After our emotional check-in, we'll delve into each sign's monkey mind, exploring those daily mental checklists we craft for ourselves—the little things we do without necessarily meaning to.

Our adventure then turns to a part of everyday life that some might relish (hello Capricorn) and others might resist (hello Pisces), but one we simply cannot skip: work!

Finally, we'll guide you back into the arms of Morpheus, god of dreams, concluding the day by exploring how each sign drifts off to sleep.

THE SIGNS WAKING UP

Let's peel back the covers, so to speak, and unveil the morning routines, habits, and quirks of each zodiac sign as they arise from their dreams and step into consciousness. From the early risers who are up at the crack of dawn with boundless energy, to the not-so-morning people, such as Taurus and Cancer, who cling to the warmth of their beds long past the sound of the alarm, and finally, to those who begin the day with their mind already spinning around the block, our beloved air signs.

Each sign has its unique way of facing the morning, from the brief moment of grogginess to the burst of inspiration, and even the practical considerations that guide them through their daily routines. Some signs might grumble at the thought of leaving their dreams behind, while others embrace the dawn with open arms.

BEGINNERS: Look at your Sun sign.

TAKE THINGS DEEPER: Look at your rising sign. As the name suggests, your "rising" sign can show how you rise!

The rising sign, also known as the 1st house cusp or the ascendant, is often described as how we are perceived by the world and how we present ourselves to the world. Indeed, the rising sign shows how we "materialize" and the energy we lead with. When you enter a room, and no one knows who you are, typically the energy that others pick up on is your rising sign. Think of it as your representative!

The rising sign is how you "materialize" yourself and marks the point of transition from the immaterial to the material. We can think of it as the point of transition from womb to birth and also the point of transition from sleep to consciousness.

The Zodiac Signs Waking Up

Capricorn
5:00 a.m.

Everyone knows true winners are part of the 5 a.m. club.

Aquarius
7:00 a.m.

I refuse to get out of bed because the alarm rang and I won't be told what to do.

Cancer
8:00 a.m.

Wake up with the sheet tattooed on my puffy cheek. Must cuddle something immediately, or ELSE.

Taurus
8:30 a.m.

Grumpily emerge. Not happy about it but will nap it out later.

Pisces
8:45 a.m.

I was actually lucid dreaming and chose to wake up. After 13 hours.

Aries
6:00 a.m.
Ready to FIGHT. Let's get it, winner!

Leo
6:30 a.m.
Rise and shine, you beautiful beast! Singing while having coffee.

Virgo
6:45 a.m.
Open one eye and am immediately hit by a wave of anxiety my morning coffee will only bring up a notch.

Gemini
7:15 a.m.
Immediately open social media before my second eyelid is open. Texted my bestie within 20 seconds.

Aquarius
7:25 a.m.
Fine. I do need to pay the bills, I guess.

Libra
7:30 a.m.
First things first: What outfit am I wearing today?

Sagittarius
9:00 a.m.
Instantly in a good mood, probably because I am still drunk from last night.

Scorpio
12:00 p.m.
I live at night so I wake up only now and won't open the blinds before 3 p.m. That's the law.

THE SIGNS' PYRAMID OF NEEDS

In this series, we draw inspiration from Maslow's pyramid of needs to craft a zodiac sign pyramid of desires. Abraham Maslow, the renowned twentieth-century psychologist, sculpted the pyramid of needs with three tiers: at the base lie our fundamental needs, at the summit are our self-fulfillment needs (a fancy way of saying, what we need to become the best version of ourselves), and sandwiched in the middle, our psychological needs.

In the following section, we'll sprinkle some stardust on his model as we playfully unravel what truly floats the boat of each zodiac sign.

BEGINNERS: Look at your Sun sign.

TAKE THINGS DEEPER: Look at your Moon sign. In astrology, Moon represents your feminine self and, in a sense, your underbelly. While Sun represents your identity, your vital force, your vitality, and your ego, Moon represents who you are when no one is looking, what you need to feel safe, nurtured, happy, and content.

Moon represents our emotional needs, our relationship to our emotions and how we feel and respond to them, and to a great extent, it represents the compass we must follow to feel regulated, happy, and thriving. For example, Libra Moon simply cannot thrive in conflict and chaos, needing a lot of balance, coregulation, and relationships to survive and thrive, while Aries Moon is more than happy to have confrontation and conflict—if anything, it's a drive to conquer and win!

The Moon's placement in your chart serves as a guide to understanding what truly makes you feel at home and emotionally satisfied. So, when exploring your core needs, pay close attention to the Moon—it holds the key to unraveling your profound emotional landscape and fundamental needs.

ARIES

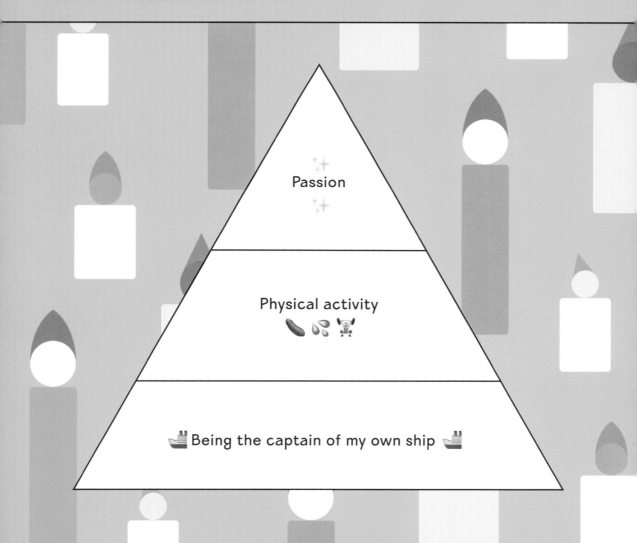

Passion

Physical activity
🥒 💦 🏋️

🚢 Being the captain of my own ship 🚢

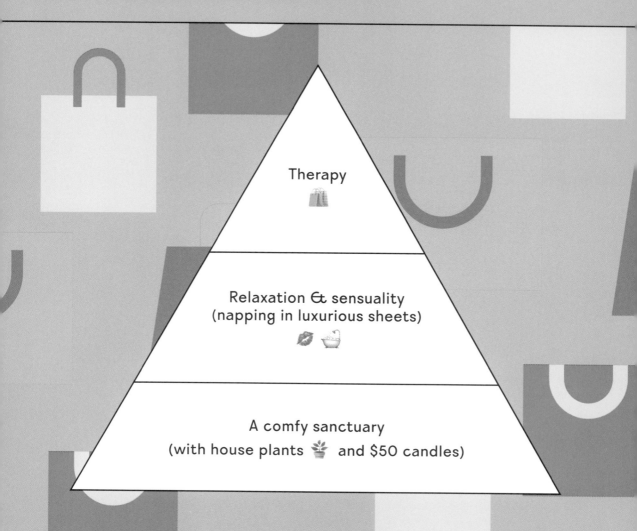

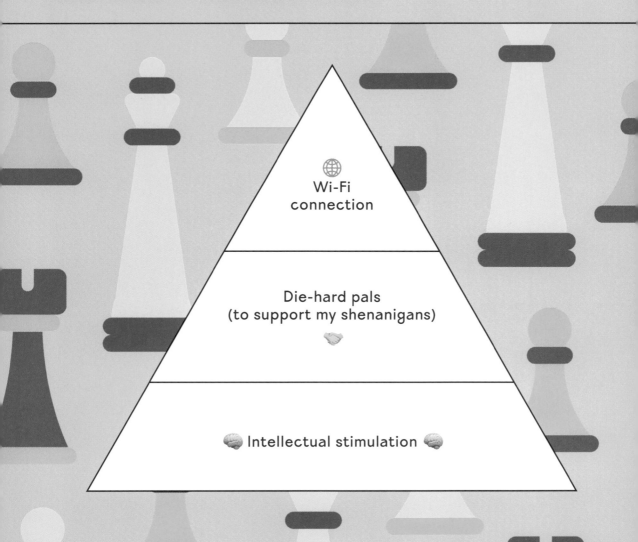

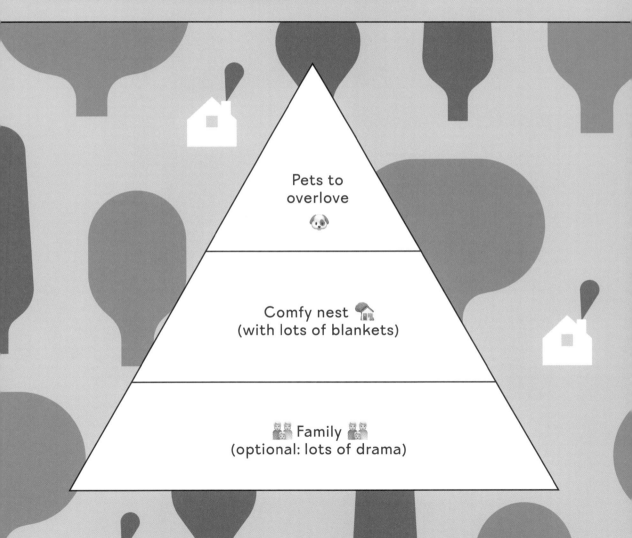

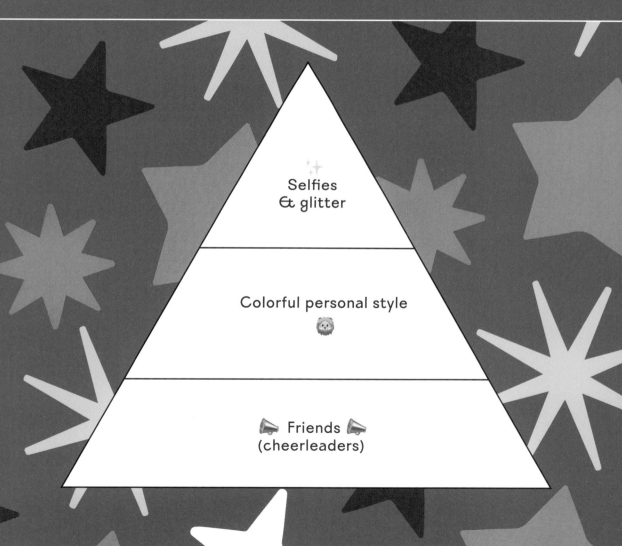

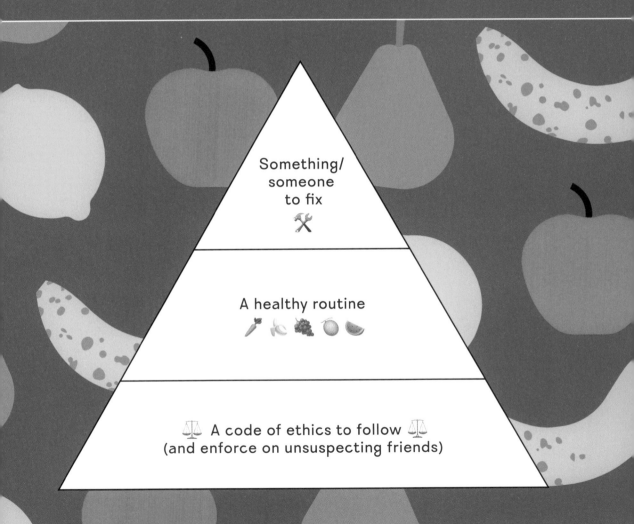

LIBRA

HIERARCHY
OF
NEEDS

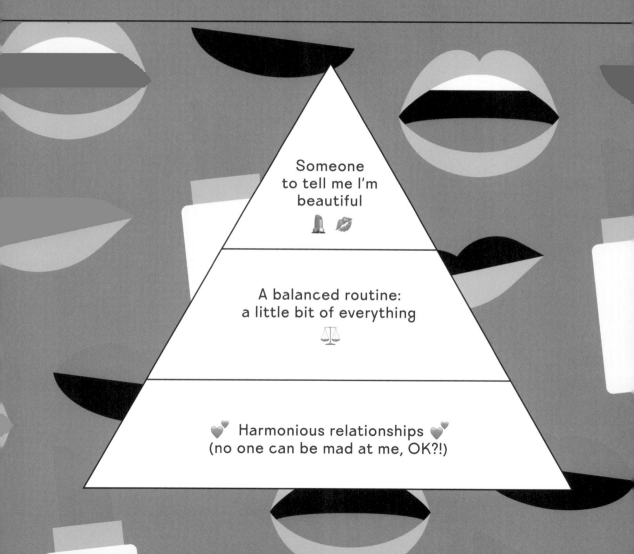

SCORPIO

HIERARCHY
OF
NEEDS

🗡️ A little bit
of an edge

👁️ Privacy 👁️
(while I actively seek to
infringe on that of others)

Deep and intimate relationships
(while I resist every attempt to form them)
🩶🩶

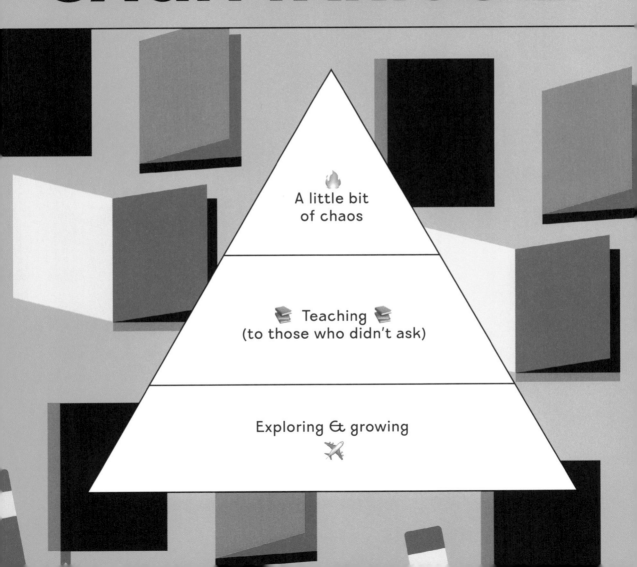

CAPRICORN HIERARCHY OF NEEDS

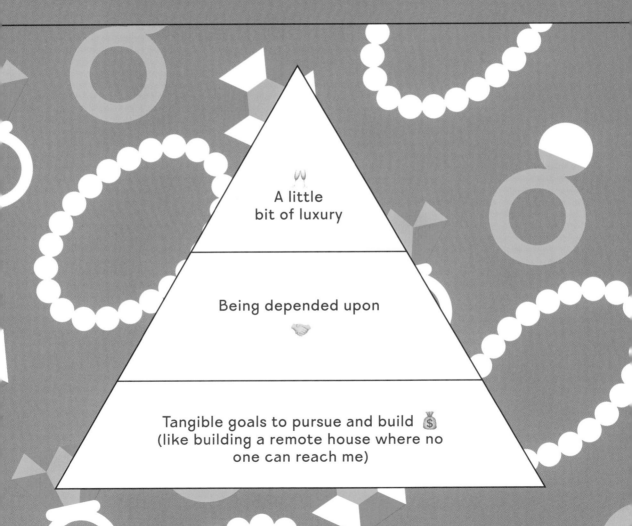

A little
bit of luxury

Being depended upon

Tangible goals to pursue and build 💰
(like building a remote house where no
one can reach me)

AQUARIUS

👽
Conspiracy
theories
Eccentric opinions

Freedom 🕊️
(to be defined as: doing whatever I
please, whenever I please, at all times)

🏙️ Community 🏙️
(of intelligent people, PLEASE)

PISCES

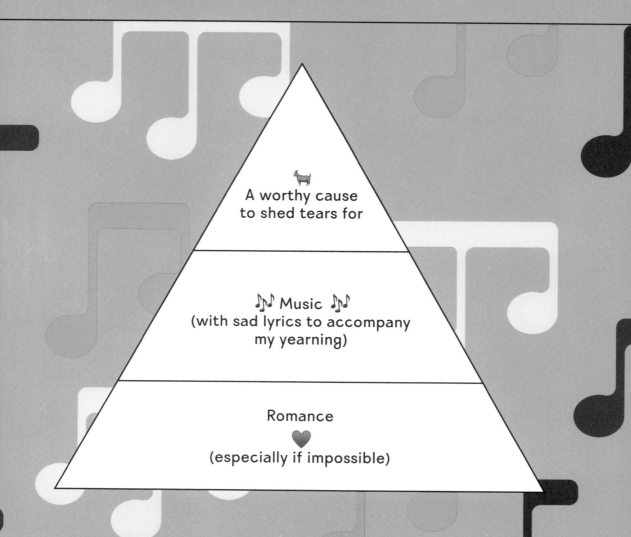

THE SIGNS' DAILY CHECKLISTS

You know those little things we all do, almost on autopilot, from the moment we open our eyes in the morning—rituals, habits, ticks that we just can't help?

In this series, we'll take a look inside each zodiac's day-to-day checklist—one they never wrote, yet probably follow every day.

BEGINNERS: Look at your Sun sign.

TAKE THINGS DEEPER: Look to Mercury. Mercury in the birth chart is associated with communication, intellect, and the way an individual processes information. It represents how we express ourselves verbally, our cognitive abilities, and our approach to learning and problem-solving.

The position of Mercury in the birth chart can shed light on an individual's communication style, thinking patterns, and areas of intellectual interest. In essence, Mercury is your monkey mind, the inner wiring of your brain, and how you tend to think.

Aries Daily Checklist

o Get in a workout

o Carry the burden of being the absolute best at everything

o Get mad at slow walkers/drivers

o Take a risk

o Be hot

o Start many things, finish none

o Curse my enemies

Taurus Daily Checklist

o Reject at least one request

o Load up on snacks

o Take a nap

o Wrap myself in a
  comfy hoodie

o Buy a candle

o Draw one hard boundary
  with someone (just because)

o Spend time alone,
  unbothered by anyone

Gemini Daily Checklist

- o Rationalize why I haven't done the thing I said I would

- o Multitask to the point of exhaustion

- o Prank someone

- o Deflect serious questions with jokes

- o Learn something new

- o Make sure to have 23 tabs opened at any point in time

- o Play devil's advocate just for fun

Cancer Daily Checklist

o Clock in one meltdown

o Cuddles

o Get offended by at least one harmless remark

o 15 min. of uninterrupted nostalgia

o Pet a dog

o Call mom

o Cook something for someone

o Be my bestie's therapist

Leo Daily Checklist

o Sing

o Give someone a compliment

o Catch someone staring at me in
  the store window reflection

o Spend money like it grows on a tree

o Wear something glorious

o Selfies

o Buy myself a gift

Virgo Daily Checklist

- Rehearse what-if scenarios that won't ever happen

- Silent judging

- Bask in the glory of small progress

- Clean

- Point out someone's typos

- Play therapist

- Complain sarcastically

Libra Daily Checklist

o Spend my entire day thinking about someone else

o Flirt with the cashier

o Please myself by people-pleasing

o Stretch my body just like I stretch
   my boundaries: hard!

o Selfies

o Play coy as a strategy

Scorpio Daily Checklist

- Let someone live rent-free in my head

- Dark humor jokes

- Think about life and death

- Plan revenge scenarios I won't act out

- Silent brooding

- Murder documentaries

- Snoop too deep until I hurt my feelings

Sagittarius Daily Checklist

o Make checklists

o Make sure everyone knows I'm right

o Spontaneous adventures

o Learn something new

o Offend someone with the "blunt truth"

o Fantasize about my next trip

o Be philosophical about something entirely trivial

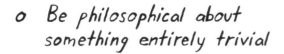

Capricorn Daily Checklist

o Work

o Make sure to exercise my right to be unimpressed and dissatisfied

o Revel in the fact that I'm definitely better than most

o Act like a parent/boss figure to people who are neither my children nor my employees

o Crush my routine

o Wear business outfits for no reason

Aquarius Daily Checklist

o Fight back against imaginary
  restrictions on freedom

o Entertain my friendships (from afar)

o Spend one hour alone uninterrupted

o Watch YouTube conspiracy theories

o Say things just to
  see how they land

o Read a good
  sci-fi book

Pisces Daily Checklist

o Listen to music and/or make music

o Fantasize about a crush (celeb or anon)

o Clock in one crying sesh

o Watch a movie (or 3)

o Free-flowing dance

o Practice my acting game in the mirror

o Respond to at least one friend I have been unintentionally ghosting for the last 3 weeks

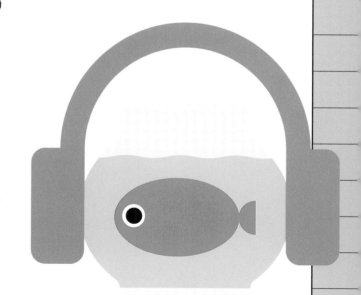

THE SIGNS AT WORK

Work is a big part of our lives (we're looking at you, Capricorns) and let's face it, we all bring a little piece of the zodiac to the daily grind. Whether you're a dynamic Aries charging into projects headfirst, a diligent Virgo dotting the i's and crossing the t's, or a charming Libra working their diplomacy magic, your sign's energy shines through at the workplace.

In this series, we're diving into the unique quirks, the strengths, and, of course, the occasional zodiac drama that each sign brings to the office water-cooler (both metaphorically and, let's be honest, probably literally). You'll find some laughs, some aha moments, and maybe even a few pointers on how to collaborate better with your zodiac colleagues.

BEGINNERS: Look at your Sun sign.

TAKE THINGS DEEPER: Look at your Mars sign. In astrology, Mars signifies energy, drive, ambition, and assertiveness, influencing how individuals take action and assert themselves in various aspects of life, including the work-place. The planet Mars governs work ethic, ambition, and leadership style, with those having a strong Mars placement often characterized by drive, motivation, and goal-oriented behavior.

To put it simply, Mars represents how we work. It's the planet associated with the masculine polarity and how we essentially approach tasks, produce results, and operate within the workplace.

Aries Workday

Be the first to arrive:
Show, don't tell
6:15 a.m.

Be the #1 superstar everyone adores, respects,
and looks up to
6:45–10:45 a.m.

Resist the urge to
impulsively quit
10:45–11:45 a.m.

Lunch break (work out for
55 minutes, eat for 5)
11:45 a.m.–12:45 p.m.

Zoom meeting (make sure
to interrupt a few times
to assert dominance)
1:00–3:00 p.m.

Team lead (I'm not, but I am)
3:00–4:30 p.m.

Taurus Workday

Recovery from waking up
7:30-9:00 a.m.

Snacks
9:00 a.m.

Work (but begrudgingly)
9:30 a.m.-12:00 p.m.

Lunch (everyone is impressed by my homemade food)
12:00-1:30 p.m.

Online shopping
1:30-2:15 p.m.

Try to make it through the Zoom meeting without having to participate
2:15-3:15 p.m.

Spend way too much time on the design part of a task
3:15-4:15 p.m.

Snacks
4:15 p.m.

Be mad about something I was told to do that I think is stupid but do it anyways (but grumpily)
4:45-6:30 p.m.

Gemini Workday

Finishing one week's worth of work in just one morning one minute before the deadline, fueled by coffee and anxiety
8:00 a.m.–12:00 p.m.

MOOD SWING
10:15 a.m.

Compulsive Google searches (don't ask)
12:00 p.m.

Launching a rumor just for funsies
5:15–6:15 p.m.

Sending a slightly passive-aggressive email (not mad, just bored)
4:15–5:15 p.m.

Multitasking into oblivion
2:15–4:15 p.m.

Lunch & gossip
12:30–1:30 p.m.

Duolingo
1:30 p.m.

Cancer Workday

Nurturing relationships with clients, coworkers, and bosses
8:00–9:30 a.m.

Passive-aggressive emails
9:30–11:00 a.m.

Pet the office dog
11:00 a.m.

Home-cooked lunch (made some extra in case someone was hungry)
12:00–1:00 p.m.

Misinterpreting someone's tone
1:00 p.m.

Cry in the bathroom
1:30 p.m.

Human bonding time
2:00–4:00 p.m.

Mood swings
4:00–4:45 p.m.

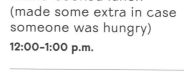

Leo Workday

STAGE ENTRANCE
8:00 a.m.

Team Lead (making everyone feel seen and validated with carefully crafted praise)
8:45–11:15 a.m.

Tag my boss in an Instagram story calling them "the best the company has ever seen"
11:15 a.m.–12:15 p.m.

Iconic lunch (i.e., telling everyone about my glamorous adventures of the past weekend)
12:15–1:15 p.m.

Start some drama
2:00 p.m.

Deny starting the drama
2:30 p.m.

Post a selfie
3:15 p.m.

Lead the Zoom meeting like it's the Super Bowl halftime
4:00–5:00 p.m.

STAGE EXIT
6:00 p.m.

Virgo Workday

Annoyed
7:00 a.m.–12:00 p.m.

Find typos in other people's work
9:00–11:00 a.m.

Judge everyone's meal (the THINGS people put in their bodies)
12:00–12:45 p.m.

Collect napkins to stuff into my car's glove compartment
12:45 p.m.

Spiral into shame (no prompt needed)
1:30–2:15 p.m.

Spend three hours on a project that supposedly requires one because they don't understand I'm detail-oriented and that's how you get proper work done
2:15–5:15 p.m.

Annoyed again
5:15 p.m.

Libra Workday

Fashionably late entrance
9:00 a.m.

Redecorating the office
9:45–10:30 a.m.

Team-building (flirting)
10:45 a.m.–12:00 p.m.

**Lunch & gossip sharing
and gathering**
12:00–12:45 p.m.

**Talking people into doing my
job without them realizing it**
12:45–6:00 p.m.

Outfit change
6:30 p.m.

Scorpio Workday

Plotting a hostile takeover
8:00-9:30 a.m.

Intense, focused work (close blinds and lock the door)
9:30-10:30 a.m.

Intimidate coworkers with *the death stare*
10:30 a.m.-12:00 p.m.

Intel gathering at lunch
12:00-1:00 p.m.

Casually stalking a frenemy
1:00 p.m.

Be my coworkers' unpaid therapist
1:30-3:00 p.m.

Spy on competition
3:00-4:00 p.m.

Meeting (make a dark joke simply for the shock value)
4:00-6:00 p.m.

Sagittarius Workday

Hangover recovery
7:30–9:15 a.m.

Make sure to be the clown-in-chief at the Zoom meeting
9:15–10:15 a.m.

Research flight tickets
10:15–11:30 a.m.

Work on my vision board
11:30 a.m.–12:30 p.m.

Boozy lunch with the crew
12:30–1:30 p.m.

Teaching people who supposedly know how to do their job how to TRULY do their job
2:00–4:30 p.m.

HR meeting
(apparently swearing
at coworker is against
company's policy?)
4:30–5:30 p.m.

Capricorn Workday

Actual efficient work (obviously, someone has to do it)
6:30–10:15 a.m.

Plotting world domination
10:30 a.m.–12:00 p.m.

Lunch break (& check stocks)
12:00–12:45 p.m.

Rubbing shoulders with corporate executives (eyes on the prize!)
12:45 p.m.

Meetings & presentations (crushing them, obviously)
1:00–3:00 p.m.

Plotting world domination (continued)
3:15–4:45 p.m.

Silently judging everyone's work ethic
4:45 p.m.

Retirement planning
5:30 p.m.

After-work networking
6:00–7:00 p.m.

Aquarius Workday

Problem-solving with the team (they don't know it's a problem yet, but I do)
7:00–9:45 a.m.

Resenting how tasks assigned are dumb, ineffi-cient, and beneath me
10:15 a.m.–12:00 p.m.

Lunch break (& convince everyone UFOs and astrology ARE real)
12:30–1:30 p.m.

Work (. . . on pretending I'm not smarter than "the boss")
2:00–4:45 p.m.

Coffee break (networking)
3:00–3:45 p.m.

Working on side hustle
5:00–6:00 p.m.

Pisces Workday

Daydreaming about an imaginary world where my soulmate is hand-feeding me strawberries while I'm lying naked on the back of a pony
9:00–10:45 a.m.

Do some creative work
11:00 a.m.–12:00 p.m.

Musical lunch break
12:00–1:00 p.m.

Look for the next concert to attend
1:15 p.m.

Yearning
2:00–3:00 p.m.

Rush to finish the project for which the deadline is tonight at midnight
3:00–7:30 p.m.

Meditation break
4:00 p.m.

Crush on coworker
5:00–5:45 p.m.

THE SIGNS GOING TO SLEEP

We've concluded our days and now it's time to put the zodiac signs to bed, as we explore their nightly routines and the thoughts that occupy their minds as they surrender to the embrace of Morpheus, the god of dreams.

From Aries, whose competitive nature doesn't even spare their dreams, to Pisces, who drifts into a world of fantasy with ease, we'll explore how these celestial personalities bid farewell to the waking world for a night's rest. Do Leo's dreams mirror their grand ambitions? Does Virgo make to-do lists in their sleep? What mysteries do Scorpio's dreams hold? These questions and more will be unveiled as we dive into the world of the zodiac signs as they venture into the realm of dreams.

BEGINNERS: Look at your Sun sign.

TAKE THINGS DEEPER: Look at your Moon sign and/or the zodiac sign located in your 12th house. As the house preceding the 1st house—the house of self—the 12th house becomes a threshold between wakefulness and the dream state. Just as the rising sign can show how you rise into consciousness, the 12th house represents the opposite experience: the fall into unconsciousness, our nighttime dream state. The 12th house encompasses the experiences of falling asleep, dreams, and the subconscious processes that unfold during rest.

The Zodiac Signs Going To Bed

Capricorn

10:00 p.m.

The world belongs to those who wake up early.

Libra

11:00 p.m.

Not too early, not too late, right in the middle: I need my beauty sleep.

Leo

11:15 p.m.

One last luscious hair treatment and I'll be ready to sleep in my 1,000-thread-count sheets.

Aries

11:30 p.m.

Don't feel like sleeping but gotta run the show tomorrow again, being the best the earth has ever seen.

Sagittarius

12:30 a.m.

Party ended early. I guess I shall rest for another day of shenanigans.

Pisces

1:00 a.m.

I just needed to finish bingeing this show. Now I can rest.

Virgo

10:30 p.m.

I have a long day of overthinking tomorrow. Better tuck myself in early.

Cancer

10:50 p.m.

One last scroll on my ex's IG profile and I swear I'll sleep.

Taurus

11:35 p.m.

One last add-to-cart and then I'll sleep, I swear.

Gemini

11:45 p.m.

All that letting my intrusive thoughts win truly did exhaust me. Time to sleep.

Aquarius

?

I know no master. I shall sleep whenever I decide.

Scorpio

3:00 a.m.

Just like a bat, I thrive in the dark.

2

The Zodiac Signs Do Fun & Leisure

After accompanying the zodiac signs through their day-to-day routines, it's time to usher them into a realm of well-deserved rest and recreation. Welcome to the cosmic playground of leisure and fun, where the stars guide the zodiac signs in their pursuit of joy, wellness, and relaxation—whether they are exploring the world, working out, splurging on a favorite indulgence, or surfing the internet.

We'll begin by joining the signs on vacation. Discover who is the ideal travel companion and who might test the limits of your friendship during a trip.

Then we'll head to the gym to see which signs are restored through energetic workouts and which are more likely to be posing for themselves in the mirror.

Next, we'll delve into the world of financial health. When it comes to money instinct, who's the savvy saver, the spontaneous splurger, or the careful budgeter? As we navigate the celestial landscape of spending habits, these insights might illuminate your own relationship to financial matters.

Finally, we'll enter the virtual realm where astrological identity plays a role in shaping online adventures. From witty comments to social media escapades, the zodiac signs each have their own way of exploring the vast internet landscape.

THE SIGNS ON VACATION

Let's whisk the zodiac signs away on a well-deserved vacation. In this chapter, we'll explore each sign's vacation habits and see how they choose to rejuvenate their minds, bodies, and spirits. Who prefers to lounge at an expensive resort? Who opts for a cozy cabin in the mountains? And when it comes to planning, who is most likely to embark on an impromptu road trip, and who is devoted to meticulously planned itineraries?

We'll dive into the signs' suitcases to see who overpacks in preparation for any and every scenario and who always seems to forget essential items.

As the zodiac signs embark on journeys near and far, we'll slip into their carry-on as they set out on spontaneous road trips or follow carefully curated itineraries. The vacation habits of the zodiac signs promise a delightful journey through the lens of astrology.

BEGINNERS: Look at your Sun sign.

TAKE THINGS DEEPER: Look to your Venus sign. In astrology, Venus represents love, beauty, harmony, and the way individuals relate to pleasure and leisure. When considering its influence on relaxation and vacation preferences in the birth chart, Venus plays a significant role in shaping one's enjoyment of downtime and aesthetic preferences.

Venus's connection to socializing and relationships also influences vacation preferences. Some may prioritize romantic getaways, while others may find joy in spending quality time with friends and loved ones. The pursuit of pleasure and indulgence is characteristic of Venus, so those with a prominent Venus influence in their birth chart may find themselves gravitating toward activities like spa retreats, fine dining, and lavish cultural experiences.

ARIES ON VACATION

Extreme sports	Must drive something really fast	Hot selfies	Clocks in some gym time	Forgot their toothbrush
Must do something different each day	Document the trip on IG stories	Almost missed the flight	THRILLS	Almost broke a bone at least once
Destination must be hot or adventurous	Local parties	♈	Stays at the hotel for 45 min. TOPS each day	Speeding tickets don't count overseas, right?
Early riser	Is the one in charge of the program	Almost got into a fight	Off-road adventures	TEQUILA SHOTS
Sponta-neously extends the trip	Will probably have a holiday fling	Competitive sports	Swears in the local language	Dives in the no-dive pool

TAURUS ON VACATION

Phone on DND the whole time	Daily naps	SPA	Tries every local food	Overweight suitcase
Either at a 5-star hotel or in a humble tree house	Do NOT wake them up or else	Did not forget a single item	Brought 5 perfumes just in case	Fine dining
Must have daily lazing around time	Most appreciative of high-quality sheets	♉	At the airport 3 hours in advance	Every day is already prescheduled as per detailed program
Gained 5 lbs	All-you-can-eat buffets	Never skips breakfast	Nature trips	Reads books on a lounge chair
The art of relaxation mastered	"Hey, it's your boss, I was wondering if"–NO	Has their routine set by day 2	Actually knows how to smell the roses	Has 45 outfits packed for a 7-day trip

GEMINI ON VACATION

Facetimes friends all day	Has learned the language by end of trip	Makes 10 new friends	Stays at multiple hotels for "variety"	Eavesdrops on the guided tour nearby
Reads 3 new books	Everything is spur of the moment	Has to go to at least one museum	Bored if inactive for longer than 23 minutes	Brings home random objects
At a new bar every night	Changes their itinerary 4 times	♊	Catches their flight 1 minute before doors close	Talked to 126 strangers
Came back home with a new personality	Actually cares about local tours	Picked up local slang without even trying	Responds to emails while texting friends while on a tour bus	Keeps their followers posted with daily stories
Restless Tourist Syndrome	Last-minute itinerary change	Gets braids or a new hair color	The THRILL of bargaining at the local market	Must be doing 5 different activities a day

CANCER ON VACATION

Really appreciates the comfy pillows	Enjoys a calm vacation	Probably rescued a local stray animal	Makes it a point to only eat local food	Definitely packed an emergency kit
"Did you put your sunscreen on?"	Company matters more than the location	"Stranger danger" at least once per day	Brought medication for every possible ailment	Enjoys living at some local family's house
Packs everyone sandwiches for lunch	Easily bonds with locals	♋	Pre-cleans the room for the cleaner	Has found their routine by day 2
Won't be found in a dangerous location	Water activities	Homesick if the stay is too long	Buys gifts for loved ones	Brings back souvenirs for everyone
MOOD SWINGS	Has an emotional moment looking at the ocean	Finds locals rude	Makes everything *romantic*	Needs daily alone recharge time

LEO ON VACATION

Finally a reason to wear all those dazzling outfits	Will snap every single moment of this vacation	Only stays at the best of the best	Discovers local art	Clubbing
LUXURY	Must be in charge of the program OR ELSE	There has to be an infinity pool at some point	Has to tan thoroughly for those selfies	Tries all the hyped restaurants
The loud one in the place	Will buy designer items if they're cheaper	♌	Definitely will attempt to get a free upgrade	Overpriced cocktails
Either goes to a show or IS the show	SPA days	Is the most obnoxious yet the most liked client everywhere	Is it a vacation or is it content creation?	Brings back gifts for everyone
Temper tantrum	Asked for the manager at least once	Fancy hotel lobbies	"Am I the drama? Is it me?"	Expensive sports

VIRGO ON VACATION

Pre-trip anxiety	"Do not drink the water here. It's not filtered"	Thorough packing checklist	Detailed itineraries	Has checked the internet reviews of everything
Pre-cleans for the cleaning staff	Will probably get food poisoning	Did not forget a single item	Either neatly packed suitcases or complete & utter chaos	Inspects the sheets' cleanliness
Will def leave a review for every place they visited	High standards, but if met, deep appreciation	♍	Has a precise daily budget	Every day is already prescheduled as per detailed program
"Do you have gluten-free options?"	Nature-oriented trips	Refuses to go in the pool because it's gross	Simple pleasures and moments	Kind of disappointed by everything
Actually fills out the feedback forms	Has mastered perfect simple outfits with linen & luxury cotton	*Reapplies sunscreen*	Has mapped out the entire city before going	Post-trip anxiety

LIBRA ON VACATION

A little bit of everything every day	Finally an opportunity to wear all those outfits	SPA	Loves a cute boutique hotel	Playful all day every day
Everything in moderation (except flirting)	Charms their way into a room upgrade	Loves discovering local culture	Goes to restaurants more for the *atmosphere*	Dancing & parties
Definitely packed way too many outfits	Can't just pick 1 meal & hopes you will share	♎	At the airport a reasonable amount of time before departure	Has a loose idea of the program but nothing too set either
Will have a vacay romance	"I don't know what to wear"	"They were definitely flirting with me, right?"	Prefers if someone else would take the lead	Nothing better than shopping in a different country
Appreciates the local art scene	Will bring back postcards	Over-compromises to appease their traveling partner	Candlelit dinners & rose petals	Spends about 2 hours a day wondering what they want to eat

SCORPIO ON VACATION

Will absolutely NOT post ANY pictures of the trip	Adrenaline-filled activities	Must have defied death at least once	Kind of dreads having to leave the hotel room	Wears sunglasses at all times
Sweeps for hidden cameras in the room	Unafraid of ghettos because they're the real danger	Loves deep diving—in all the ways	"What's on your mind?" "Nothing"	Packed 14 all-black outfits
Won't wake up before 11 a.m.	Whatever they do, it has to be INTENSE	♏	Extreme sports	Has planned absolutely nothing
Day drinking	Interested in local subcultures & niches	Suspicious the cleaners will go through their stuff	Sleeps either 4 hours or 11 hours, no in between	Psycho-analyzes everyone for giggles
"Don't use the public Wi-Fi. It's not safe"	Spicy food, spicy cocktails, spicy underwear	Insist you delete the photo you took of them	Loves secluded Airbnbs	Religious and mystical tours

SAGITTARIUS ON VACATION

Didn't even plan to take this trip, just happened	Probably missed their flight	Probably flew while drunk	Left their bag on the plane	Stays at a hostel
SPONTA-NEOUS ADVENTURES	Trainwreck but a fun one	Super interested in ALL cultural & historical tours	Day clubbing	Will 100% hike something
Forgot their most import-ant items	Somewhat always one step away from jail	↗	Backpacking	Met someone at a bar and they're now on a side trip to Croatia
Forgot to turn off roaming, racks up a $500 phone bill	50/50 might decide to simply never come back	Learned how to swear in local language	Must be by some jungle or beach	Each day is content for future inspira-tional posts
Might come back married	The loudest, the funniest, or both, anywhere they go	"YOLO" as they down their fourth tequila shot	Somehow lost a single shoe	Dopamine-filled activi-ties every day

CAPRICORN ON VACATION

Worries about work the entire time	Only stays at respectable branded hotels	Has a somewhat rigid program ahead of time	Will definitely bargain on the hotel room price though	Will call the manager
Needs good Wi-Fi to respond to emails	At the airport 3 hours in advance	Reluctantly tips the hotel staff	Duty-free shopping	Fine dining or street food—no in-between
Low-grade guilt	Finds ways to make the vacation "productive"	♑	All-inclusive resorts	Has a checklist of landmarks they want to see
Finds sand quite inconvenient	Wakes up at 6 a.m. sharp	Splurges or cheaps out—no in-between	Can be found at the airport lounge	Does all the grooming services that are cheaper than at home
Complains about not having been upgraded to business class	"Hey, it's your boss, I was wondering if"—YES?	Packed a few prepared, well-thought-out outfits	Will order a bourbon at some point	Historical tours. The older the better

AQUARIUS ON VACATION

Found the most unique Airbnb	Prioritizes high-tech accommodations	Erratic outfits packed	Visits long-distance friends	Has zero schedule ahead of trip
Will NOT go to mainstream destinations	Befriends locals	Brought all of their tech gadgets	and 5 books	Will probably participate in a local protest
Needs variety in daily activities	Works throughout the trip	♒	At the airport at the last second	Needs high-speed Wi-Fi
At the hotel room for no more than 45 min. each day	Prefers urban destinations or open nature	Late-night stargazing	Travels with a group of friends	Tries the most atypical restaurants
Disappears randomly every day (NEEDS SPACE)	Almost became the leader of a local revolution	Festivals	Brings back the most unique souvenirs	Finds the most unique tour guides

PISCES ON VACATION

Finally a good reason to leave texts on read	Has the perfect playlist for every moment	Water activities	Missed their flight	Daydreams at the beach
Doesn't really care where they stay but make it *romantic*	Still watches their favorite shows	Got lost at least once and rescued by a local	Likely to attend a local concert	Forgot half of the items they needed
Oversleeps (finally socially approved to)	Really stops and smells the roses	♓	DAILY NAPS	Inspired by nature & beauty
Part of some sort of moon circle	Tried to rescue a stray pet	Has no idea which day it is	Daily schedule: Go with the flow	Frolicks in a field
Showed up at the wrong airport	Fantasizes about living here permanently	Beach yoga	Writes poetry by the seaside	Disappears from the club without telling anyone

THE SIGNS AT THE GYM

Welcome to the cosmic fitness center, where sweat meets the stars and celestial bodies pump iron on the gym floor. In this chapter, we follow the signs to the gym and decode how each star sign behaves.

From the determined Capricorn never missing a business opportunity, even when climbing the Stair-Master, to the precision of a Virgo here to perfect every one of their curves, the stars have a say in your workout routine.

But it's not just about the physical exertion; it's about the cosmic camaraderie that unfolds in the gym space. Who's the social butterfly striking up conversations between sets, and who's the focused Scorpio with a "don't disturb" aura? In this celestial gymnasium, every sign has its workout anthem, exercise preferences, and unique approach to breaking a sweat.

BEGINNERS: Look at your Sun sign.

TAKE THINGS DEEPER: Look at your Mars sign. As the planet of war and aggression, Mars has a lot to do with how we behave in the gym. Mars represents physical exertion, how we take on challenges, and what motivates us.

BENCH PRESS

Leo, Aries, and **Capricorn** argue about who's lifting the heaviest.

#PR #deadliftlife

MIRROR

Libra, Leo, and **Sag** pose in front of a mirror, taking photos with their phones.

What's the point of going to the gym if you aren't posting progress pics?

#belfie

MACHINES

Aquarius and **Gemini** hog the machines and scroll their socials, oblivious to those waiting for a turn.

#disconnect #staypresent #mentalhealthisimportant

DISGRUNTLED

Taurus and **Scorpio** become increasingly irritated as they wait for the machines, passive aggressively crossing their arms and tapping their feet while they pointedly gaze toward the clock.

"Ugh, why are people SO annoying."

YOGA

Pisces, **Virgo**, **Cancer**, **Libra**, find their flow in yoga class.

It's all about releasing your emotions by crying in pigeon pose.

THE SIGNS SPENDING MONEY

Let's open the wallets of the zodiac signs and take a deep look at how they handle money. We'll see how the signs break down when it comes to spending on nonessentials. We all have rent and groceries to pay for, but what about all the rest? See who is splurging on takeout, who holds out for the steepest discounts, and who is spending lavishly on their pet cat.

Beginners: Look at your Sun sign.

Take Things Deeper: Look at your Venus sign. In astrology, Venus plays a crucial role in understanding how individuals spend money. Associated with personal values, pleasures, and what we find "worth it," Venus influences our spending habits. The placement of Venus in your birth chart will help you better understand your relationship to spending: Are you a big spender, focused on luxury and material items? Are you naturally thrifty and focused on minimalism? Answers are found in your Venus sign!

The Zodiac Signs' Nonessential

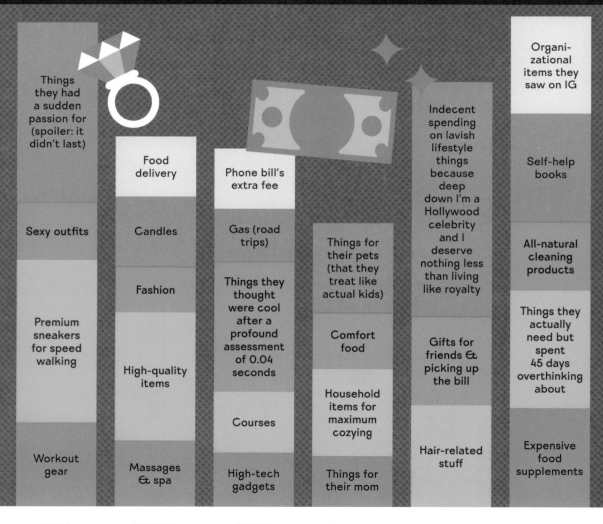

ARIES
- Things they had a sudden passion for (spoiler: it didn't last)
- Sexy outfits
- Premium sneakers for speed walking
- Workout gear

TAURUS
- Food delivery
- Candles
- Fashion
- High-quality items
- Massages & spa

GEMINI
- Phone bill's extra fee
- Gas (road trips)
- Things they thought were cool after a profound assessment of 0.04 seconds
- Courses
- High-tech gadgets

CANCER
- Things for their pets (that they treat like actual kids)
- Comfort food
- Household items for maximum cozying
- Things for their mom

LEO
- Indecent spending on lavish lifestyle things because deep down I'm a Hollywood celebrity and I deserve nothing less than living like royalty
- Gifts for friends & picking up the bill
- Hair-related stuff

VIRGO
- Organizational items they saw on IG
- Self-help books
- All-natural cleaning products
- Things they actually need but spent 45 days overthinking about
- Expensive food supplements

LIBRA	SCORPIO	SAGITTARIUS	CAPRICORN	AQUARIUS	PISCES
Birthday gifts for their many friends	Things you must never know about; why are you even asking, you nosy person?	Don't remember but was fun			Donations
Home decor	Secret investments	Exotic trips	Investments	High-quality news subscriptions	A lot of things they don't even remember
Parties & fine dining	Spy gear		Luxury items	Some spiritual subscription	
All types of clothing items, beauty treatments, nail salon & vanity-related expenses	Witchcraft things	Workshops	Things they were forced to purchase for survival purposes	Limited collection items	Several streaming service subscriptions
	Psychology books	Partying	Things bought at a HEAVY discount	The latest tech	Concert tickets

THE SIGNS ON THE INTERNET

Welcome to "The Zodiac Signs on the Internet," the ultimate cosmic exposé on your online antics! Forget about your browser history; the stars have been tracking your every click, scroll, and questionable online purchase. In this celestial journey through cyberspace, we'll uncover the digital personas of each zodiac sign, revealing the quirks, obsessions, and guilty pleasures that lurk behind the pixels.

Whether you're a secretive Scorpio lurking in the shadows of private forums, a fiery Aries engaging in comment section battles, or a diplomatic Libra curating the perfect Instagram aesthetic, the cosmos have left their mark on your virtual existence. Brace yourself for a laugh-out-loud exploration of the zodiac signs' online escapades, where astrology meets Wi-Fi, and the stars align with your search history.

BEGINNERS: Look at your Sun sign.

TAKE THINGS DEEPER: Look at your Mercury sign.

Aries on the Internet

- Uses Instagram for sliding into DMs
- Posts gym selfies
- Confronts people with "stupid" opinions in the comments
- Impulsively buys something they don't need after seeing a targeted ad
- Posts super-hot pics—it's all for the 'gram

Taurus on the Internet

- Has items in cart on at least 4 different websites at any point in time

- Perfectly controlled feed aesthetic

- IG stories mostly consist of restaurant food pics

- Finds inspiration for their home aesthetic

- Greedy with their likes

Gemini on the Internet

52 tabs opened at any point in time

13,546 emails unread

Shares and saves around 134 memes each day

Trolls people in the comments section just for giggles

Spends an inordinate amount of time googling their most random thoughts, effectively acquiring a wealth of random knowledge they'll probably never use

Cancer on the Internet

- Champions of elusive captions under sad selfies that are most definitely directed at someone

- Has a long "blocked" list

- Goes into petty comment wars with strangers

- Instagram bio is used to convey mood of the moment

- Mostly uses internet for following accounts of puppies

Leo on the Internet

- Sultry selfies

- Likes and comments on every post to show love and support to friends, family, and complete strangers

- Wishes friends happy birthday by posting photos where they low-key look better than their friend

- Crown emoji in IG bio

- Storytelling their life through content creation

Virgo on the Internet

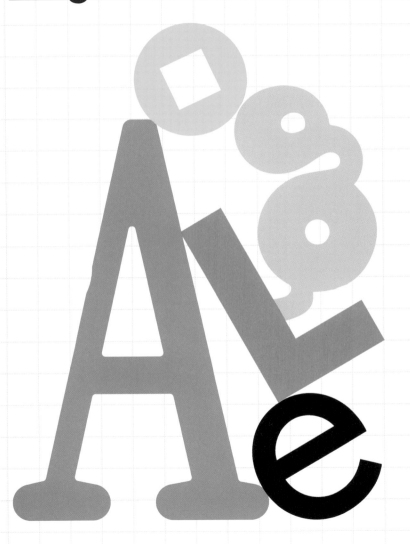

Infinite opportunities to point out grammatical errors in people's comments. What a great way to win an argument without arguing!

Anxiety-fueled, frantic googling extravaganza

Persuaded they have a terminal disease by consulting symptom checkers

Looks for home & organizational hacks

Can't help but feel like everyone is a little ridiculous online

Libra on the Internet

Mostly uses social media to lure their crush in while between relationships

Googles their situation from the perspective of the other person to see what people think

Posts their outfit of the day

Avid Reddit and Quora user (what better way to get gossip?)

Shares carefully curated memes with their friends

Scorpio on the Internet

Lurks & investigates

Not posting anything. The internet is for observation, not exposure

When they do post though, it will be cryptic and existential

Dark aesthetic

Has a bunch of side usernames for their various private interests: They won't be tracked!

Sagittarius on the Internet

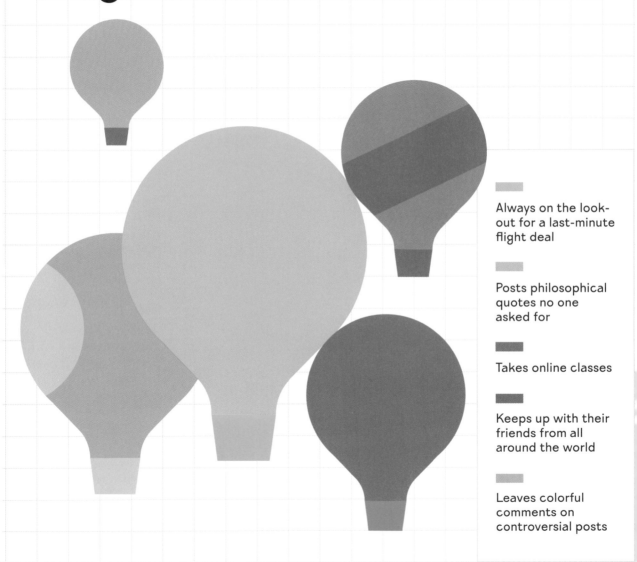

Always on the look-out for a last-minute flight deal

Posts philosophical quotes no one asked for

Takes online classes

Keeps up with their friends from all around the world

Leaves colorful comments on controversial posts

Capricorn on the Internet

Avid LinkedIn user

Mostly here for business honestly

All accounts carefully locked down and private

Watches investment strategy videos

Low-key judges everyone

Aquarius on the Internet

- DIY tutorials
- Learns new skills on YouTube
- Aware of the latest news and trends (but won't participate, obviously)
- Deactivates their accounts periodically as a digital cleanse
- Shares memes as a way to express their feelings

Pisces on the Internet

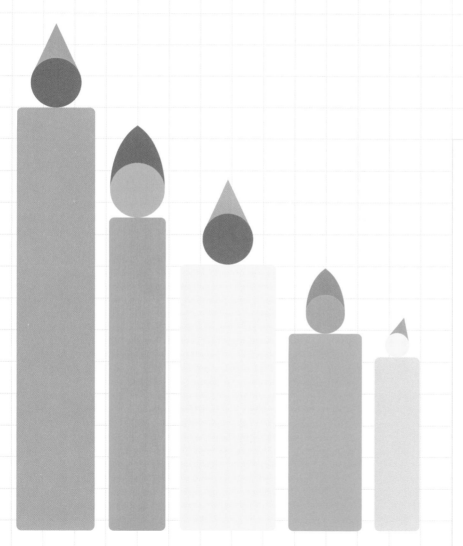

Closely follows their celeb crushes

Donates to random GoFundMe pages

Streams indie movies

Likely to join spiritual groups (and fall in love with the leader)

Doomscrolls endlessly

3

The Zodiac Signs Do Love

I present to you the juiciest part of our journey together: The zodiac signs in love and in relationships. This is without a doubt the part of our life where we think the most of the zodiac signs. We all remember our terrible relationships with a -insert zodiac sign- and we've all googled our compatibility with a partner. Even the most skeptical of us have considered whether a partner was irritating us because they're a "Gemini," right? Ah, love and relationships, our greatest joys and greatest pains.

In this chapter, we'll observe how the signs behave through all phases of relationships, whether they are swiping on dating apps, falling in (and out) of love, or settling down into a long-term partnership. We'll take a deep look under the hood of the zodiac signs and discover exactly why some zodiac signs irk us, and why we're so infatuated with others. We'll find out how your ex truly dealt with the breakup when no one was looking, and how you behave when your little heart starts to beat for someone.

THE SIGNS ON DATING APPS

In this section, we're diving into the wild playground of online dating. Whether you're a committed swiper or someone who's sworn off the apps for good, chances are you've taken a spin in the sometimes frustrating, sometimes hilarious, sometimes fruitful world of online matchmaking.

In this virtual landscape, where every participant has to present themselves to potential partners, the signs reveal their true nature. Picture the bold and spirited Aries swiping right with all the confidence in the world or the meticulous Virgo carefully curating the perfect bio while swiping left on ... absolutely everyone.

Read on to discover who is most likely to declare their love for canines, who is searching for a Hollywood romance, and who is most likely to post a photo from their most recent fishing expedition.

BEGINNER: Look at your Sun sign.

TAKE THINGS DEEPER: In this case, the Sun sign is the right entry point for all levels of astrology. Dating app profiles allow us to define ourselves to the world.

From the photos we choose to display to how we describe ourselves through our bio and prompts, online dating is all about identity curation. The Sun represents ego definition:

Who am I; what is my identity; where do I belong; how do I want to project myself?

Of course we've all come across a profile where the information is clearly inflated or distorted to make the person look better. This is still the realm of the Sun, as the Sun relates to ego, self-importance, and making oneself look "big."

Aries
Dating Profile

Works at: Fitness coach

About me

MUST WORK OUT. I lead an active lifestyle and need someone who shares the same values. I know what I want and I hope you do too. Let's skip the small talk and meet in person.

My biggest pet peeve:

Slow walkers.

Favorite quality in a person:

Courage

My interests

Ambition   Confidence

Sense of adventure

Gym   Being active

Taurus
Dating Profile

Works at: Interior designer

About me

Plant parent. Slight shopping addiction.
I'm laid-back, looking for a nondramatic
partner who understands boundaries.

A pro and con of dating me:

Pro: I'm the nonchalant one you
always dreamed of dating.
Con: You might actually miss your crazy ex.

I spend most of my money on:

Food

My interests

Dining Time offline Foodie

Sleeping well Gardening

Gemini
Dating Profile

Works at: Marketing

About me

Please don't be boring.
I speak 5 languages. I love comedy.
I read a lot of books. I need a lot of
stimulation. Looking for someone who's
exciting and down for adventures
and is constantly wanting to grow
and also someone who laughs at my
jokes (please do). MUST BANTER.

My real-life superpower is:

Knowing a little bit about everything.

We're the same type of weird if:

You google your every thought.

My interests

Comedy Road trips Museums

Reading Intelligence

Cancer
Dating Profile

Works at: Nursing

About me

I really don't want to be here. My friends and family are everything, so you'll have to seduce them as much as me!

Love my dog to death: We're a package.

Shy at first.

I'm looking for:

A reason to delete this app.

You should not go out with me if:

You're "brutally honest."

My interests

Rom-coms   Family-oriented   Empathy

Cooking   Intelligence

Leo
Dating Profile

Works at: Luxury Real Estate

About me

I am lucky to have an incredible life filled with success, purpose, love, and an amazing support network of people who are inspiring and remarkable. I'm looking for someone to add to my fabulous life. Tell me what makes you unique.

My love language:

Words of affirmation

A review from a friend:

"They're literally the best. Whoever gets to be their partner will be the LUCKIEST person on earth."

My interests

Nightlife   Being romantic   Confidence

Beaches   Ambition

Virgo
Dating Profile

Works at: Holistic health care

About me

Introvert. Likes simple things and nature.
Into clean eating, health, and fitness.
Tell me about symptoms bothering you and
I'll let you know how to improve your life!

My love language:

Acts of service.

I'm looking for:

Someone who doesn't give me the ick.

My interests

Gardening   Social awareness

Self-improvement   Camping

Nutrition

Libra
Dating Profile

Works at: Fashion

About me

I'm very self-aware and looking for someone who is similar.

I hate drama.

The key to my heart is romancing me like we're in a Hollywood movie.

Bonus: I'm a great +1 at any event.

I'll fall for you if:

You flirt with me.

Two truths, one lie:

I always know what I want for dinner.

I'm beautiful.

I'm smart.

My interests

Dining out   Intelligence   Art

Design   Positivity

Scorpio
Dating Profile

Works at: None of your business

About me

I'd love to build a really deep, meaningful, and connected relationship with someone. I'll resist every attempt to do so though.

If you want to know something, just ask.

My love language is:

Sarcasm

You should not go out with me if:

You're shallow.

My interests

Sex positivity   Adrenaline junkie

Deep chats   Horror movies

Psychology

Sagittarius
Dating Profile

Works at: Student of life

About me

Free spirit.
Brutally honest.
Traveled 43 countries and counting.
Growth-oriented & always learning.
Swipe left if you take life too seriously.

I'll fall for you if:

You can call me out on my bullsh*t.

The key to my heart:

Adventures & laughter.

My interests

Philosophy Traveling Camping

Deep chats Festivals Psychology

Capricorn
Dating Profile

Works at: CEO of myself

About me

I'm a really busy person. Looking for an ambitious and stable partner. I don't really check this app. If we match, let's schedule something asap. I'm not looking for pen pals.

I'll fall for you if:

You trip me.

What I'd like to know about you is:

Where do you see yourself in 5 years?

My interests

Ambition   Family-oriented   Intelligence

Reading   Self-development

Aquarius
Dating Profile

Works at: Freelancer

About me

Please just be weird.
Looking for a deep connection with
someone based on mutual respect &
intellectual connection. Open to friends.

Dating me is like:

Owning a cat. I will love but on my
terms and please leave the window
open, I'll come back eventually.

Favorite quality in a person:

Authenticity

My interests

Mindfulness   Human rights

Intelligence   Reading   Creativity

Pisces
Dating Profile

Works at: Musician

About me

Sensitive soul looking for a
compassionate and kind companion.
I love reading, playing guitar, and
volunteering at the local shelter.
PS: MUST BE VEGAN.

**The world would be a better place
with more:**

Love

I promise you I won't judge you if:

You cry.

My interests

Poetry   Environmentalism

Empathy   Animals   Being romantic

THE SIGNS BREAKING UP

Going through a breakup is a rite of passage, and each sign processes this basic human experience in their own unique way. Some people appear calm and collected during a breakup, while others can barely keep it together, and others rage as if the world is falling apart.

In this series, we delve into how the signs cope with the painful experiences of breakups when no one is watching. Each zodiac sign employs different strategies when it comes to dealing with their emotions and determining how open or private they are with them. Who's back on the dating apps the next day, seeking a rebound? Who's stocking up on tissues in packs of ten? Who's fleeing to New Zealand to escape reality?

BEGINNERS: Look at your Sun sign.

TAKE THINGS DEEPER: Look at your Moon sign. In astrology, the Moon represents our emotions, our needs, and how we experience and cope with emotional situations. The Moon can also signify our attachment style and how we handle breaking up with a partner.

For instance, Moon in Leo may immediately seek refuge in bold public displays of glow up and rebound, while Moon in Scorpio might prefer to keep everything concealed, healing wounds privately while perhaps fantasizing about revenge.

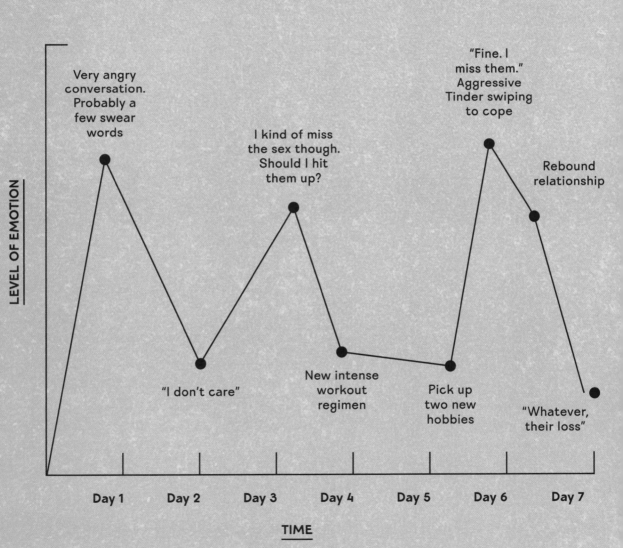

Taurus Breaking Up

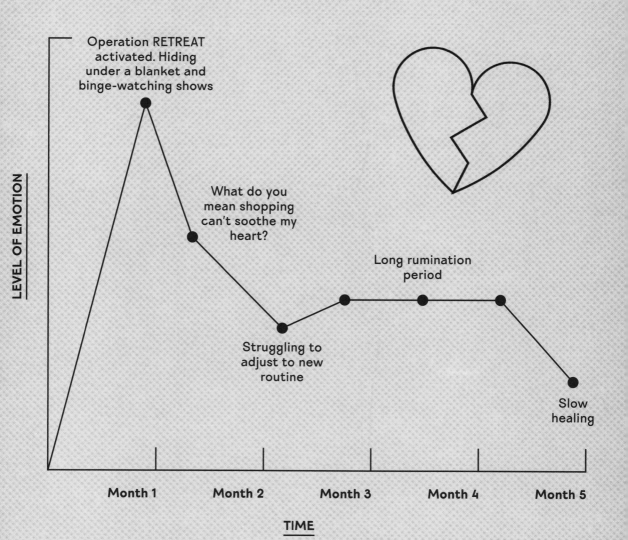

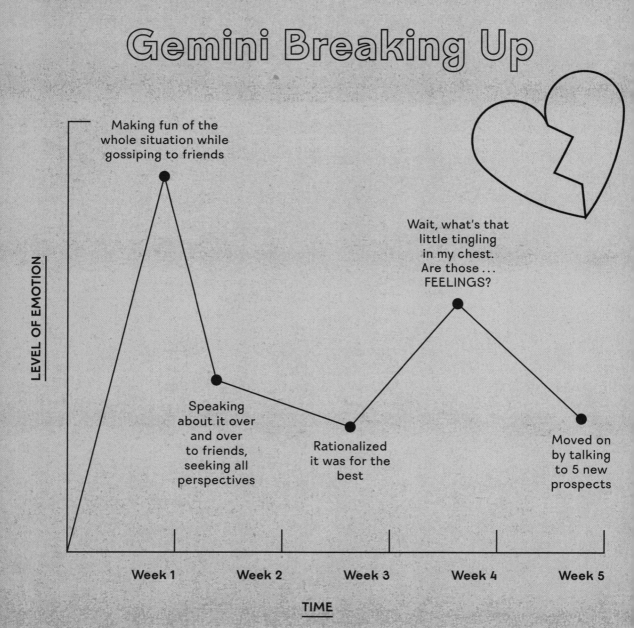

Cancer Breaking Up

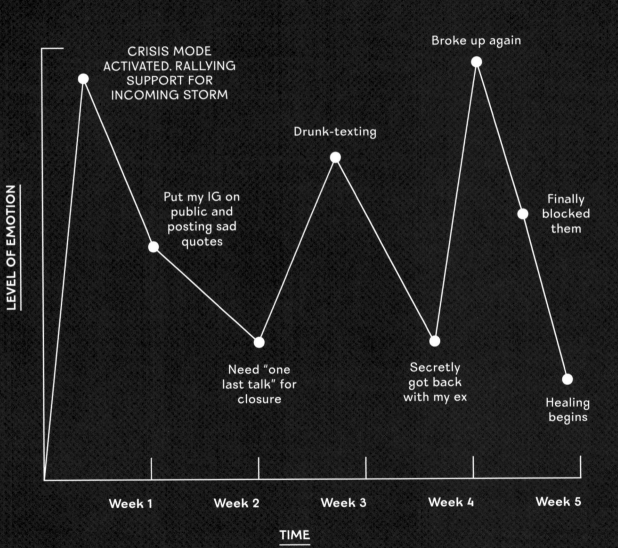

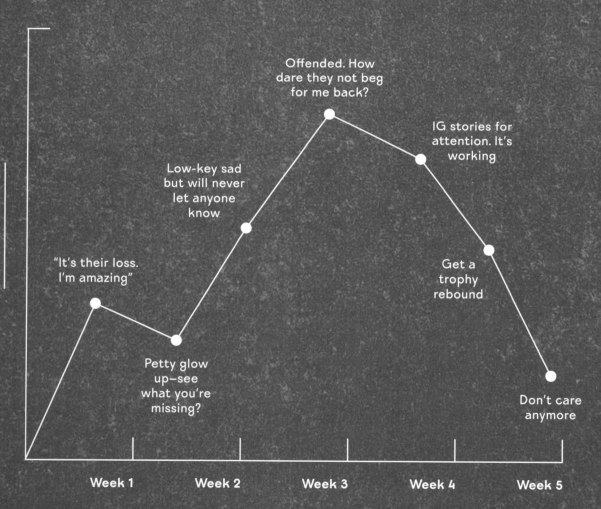

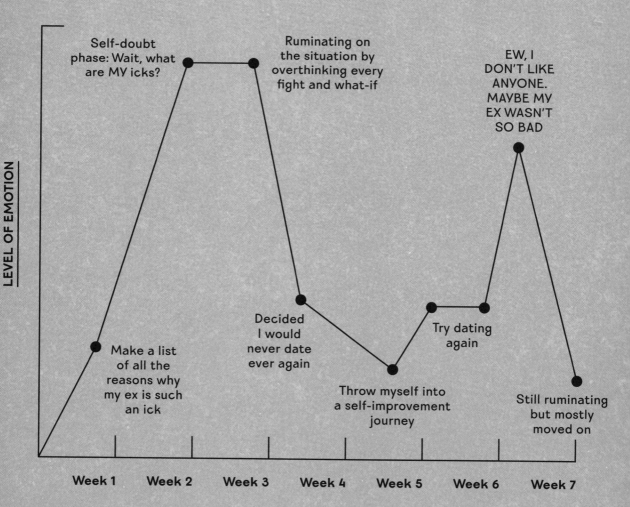

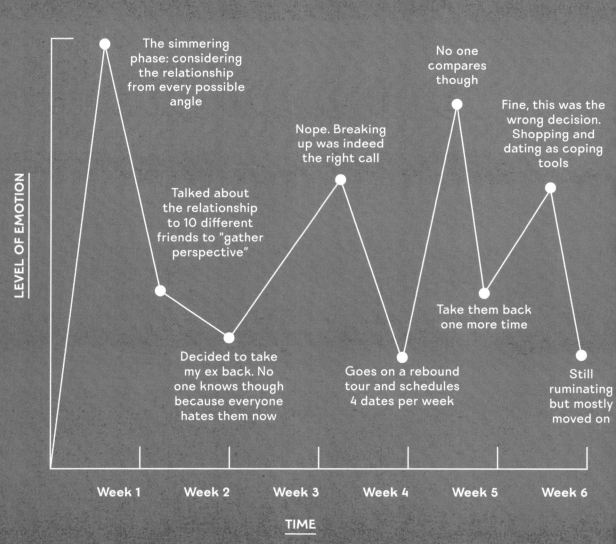

Scorpio Breaking Up

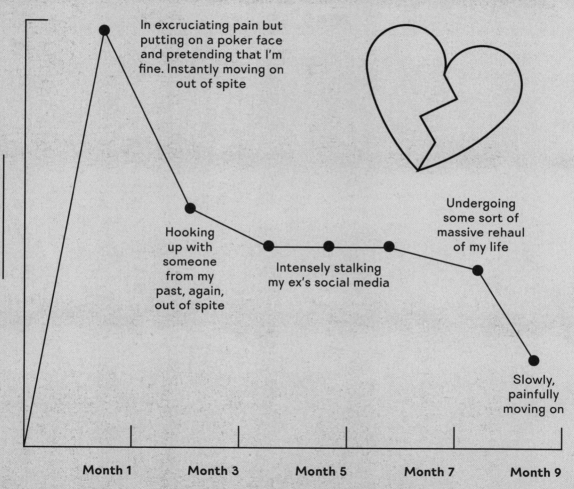

In excruciating pain but putting on a poker face and pretending that I'm fine. Instantly moving on out of spite

Hooking up with someone from my past, again, out of spite

Intensely stalking my ex's social media

Undergoing some sort of massive rehaul of my life

Slowly, painfully moving on

LEVEL OF EMOTION

Month 1   Month 3   Month 5   Month 7   Month 9

TIME

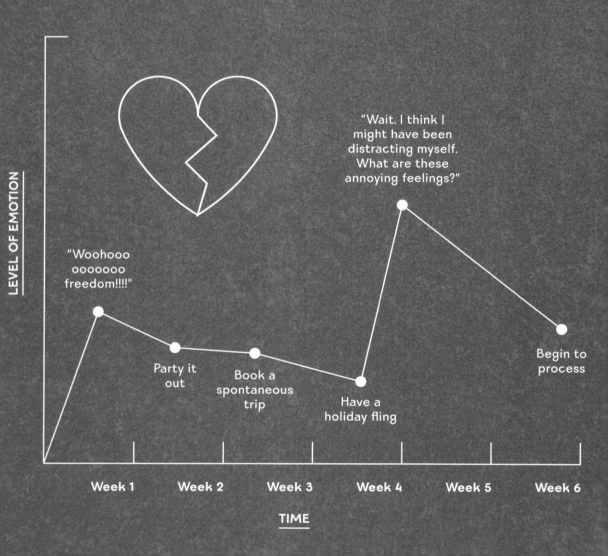

Capricorn Breaking Up

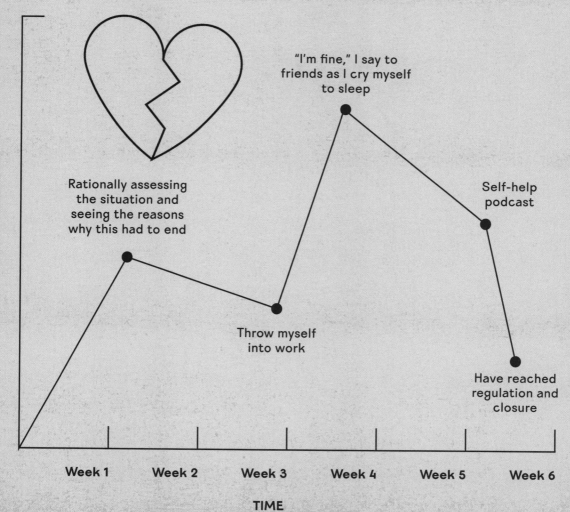

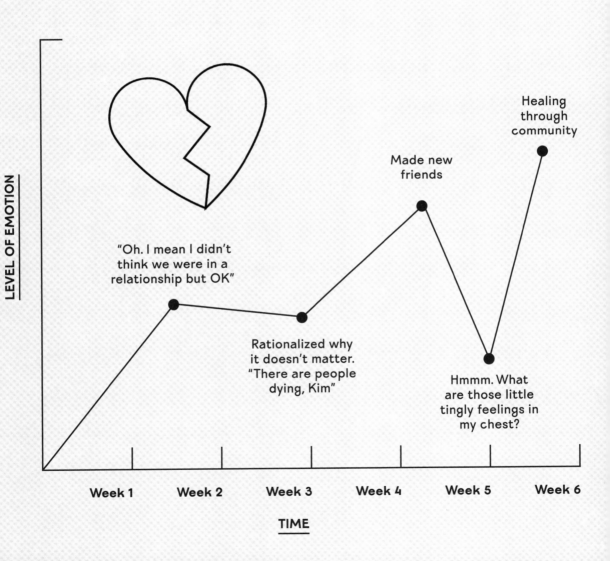

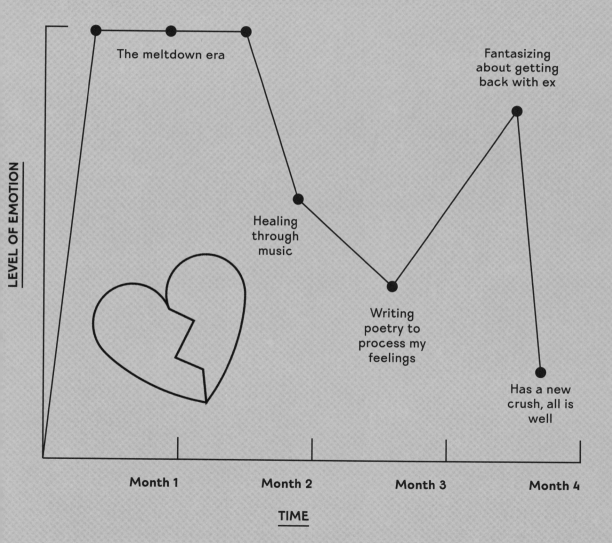

Pisces Breaking Up

LEVEL OF EMOTION

The meltdown era

Fantasizing about getting back with ex

Healing through music

Writing poetry to process my feelings

Has a new crush, all is well

Month 1   Month 2   Month 3   Month 4

TIME

THE SIGNS FALLING IN LOVE

Ah, love. Supreme anguish, delightful euphoria.

The experience of falling in love is one of the most beautiful and rewarding human experiences.

In this series, we'll explore how the zodiac signs approach the beautiful—and sometimes scary— experience of falling in love. From the neurotic and uncertain approach of Virgo to the practical and calculated ways of Taurus, we'll see how each sign navigates the realm of love and romance.

BEGINNERS: Look at your Sun sign.

TAKE THINGS DEEPER: Look at your Moon and Venus signs.

When we seek to understand how we experience love and the process of falling into it, both Moon and Venus are relevant for comprehending your unique experience.

Venus represents the attraction and infatuation we feel as we're falling in love. Venus can also represent our value system—what we find valuable, worthy, pleasant, and beautiful.

Moon represents the feeling of security that we (hopefully) feel when we find the right partner, the bonds we form, and the way we navigate feelings of vulnerability.

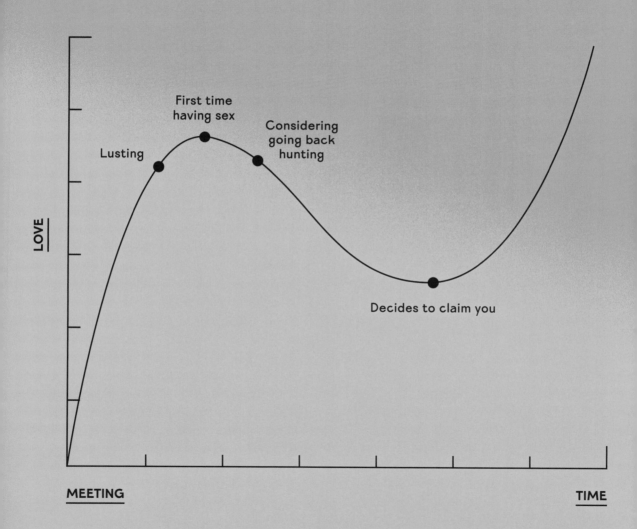

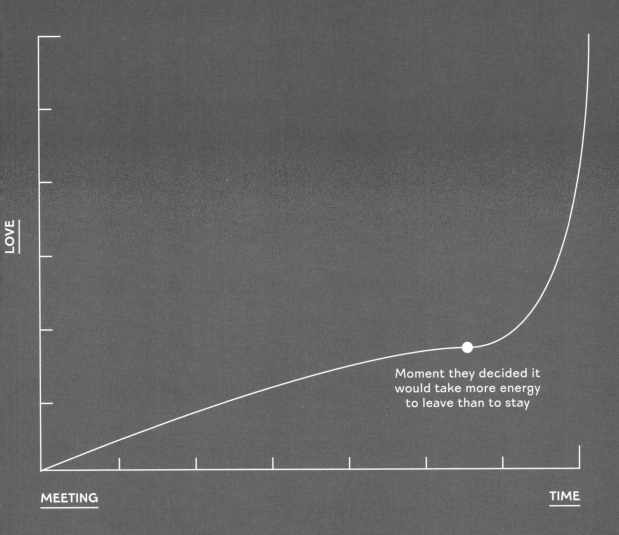

How Gemini Falls in Love

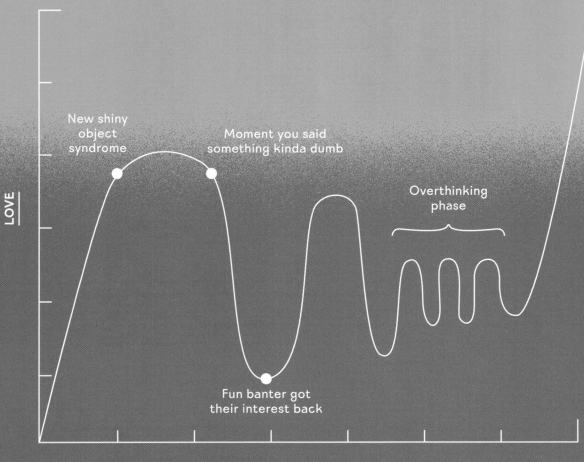

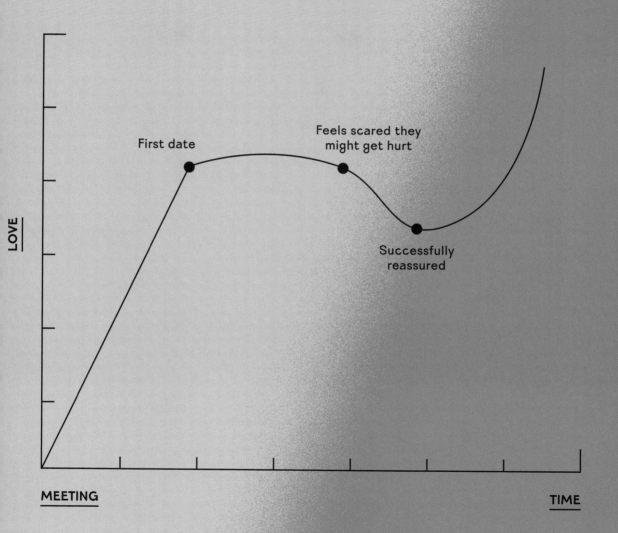

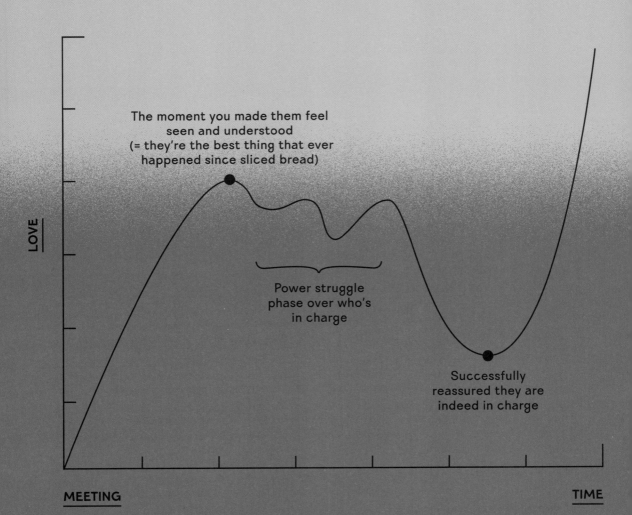

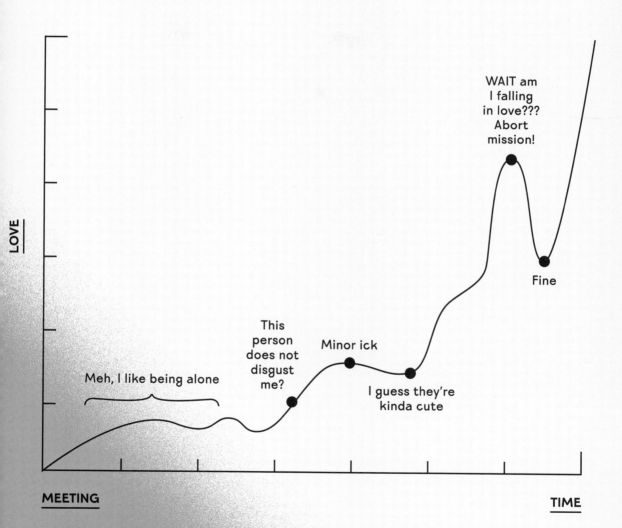

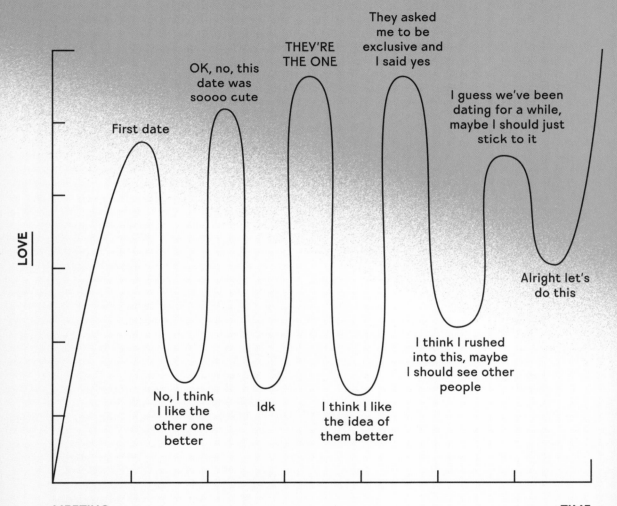

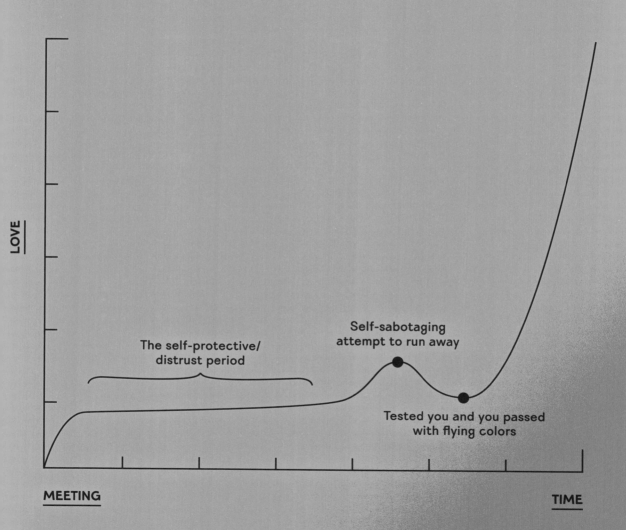

How Sagittarius Falls in Love

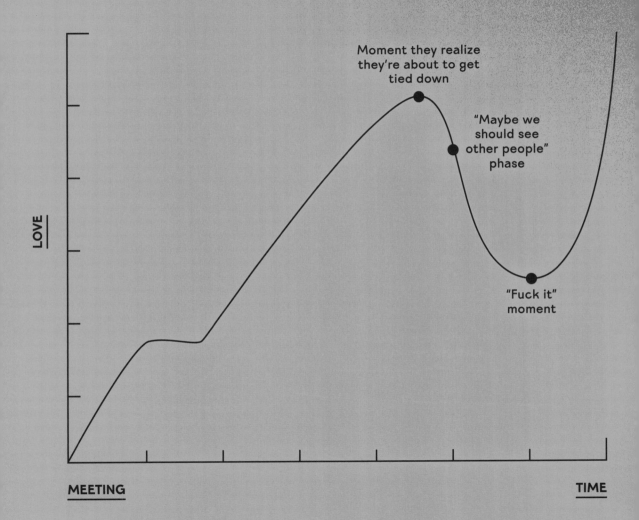

How Capricorn Falls in Love

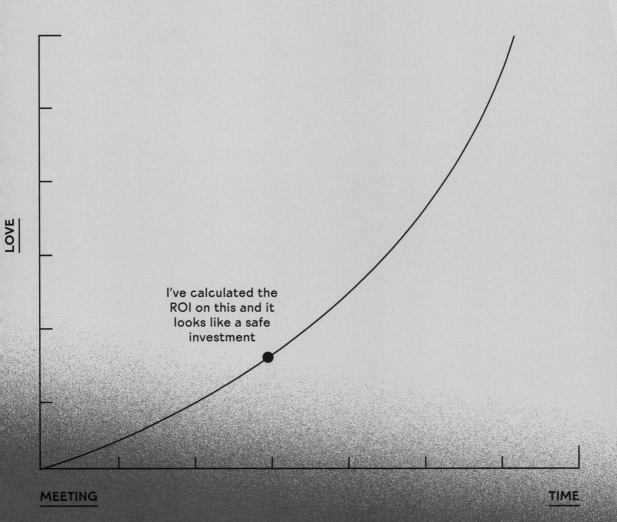

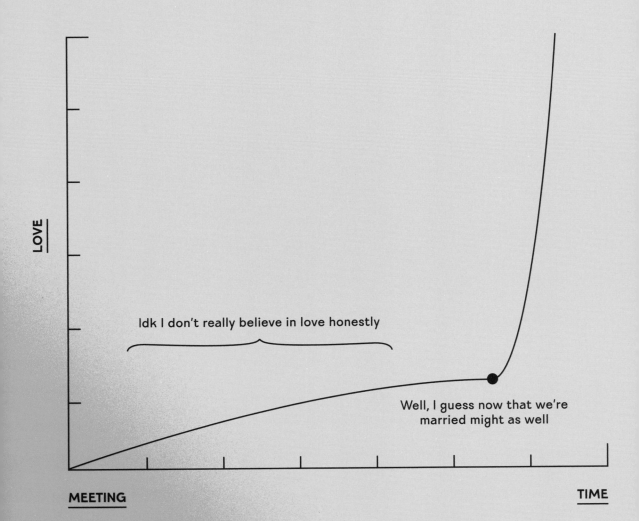

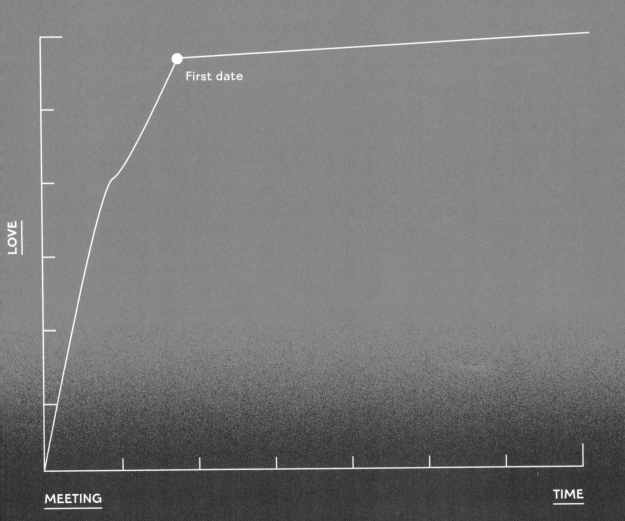

THE SIGNS IN RELATIONSHIPS

Ever caught yourself wondering what it would be like to settle down with a specific sign? Maybe it's the charming Libra coworker whom you've daydreamed about settling down with? Or the spicy Scorpio you've gone on a couple of dates with but can't get a clear read on yet...

In this series, we'll get down to the nitty-gritty of how each sign shows up in long-term partnership so that you can see who might be your cosmic match and who might just turn your world a bit topsy-turvy.

If you're already hitched, it's a chance to better understand what makes your partnership uniquely yours and how your proclivities when it comes to love, sex, communication, and more complement each other—or cause friction!

BEGINNERS: Look at your Sun sign.

TAKE THINGS DEEPER: Look at your Venus sign.

How we behave in relationships can be influenced by various factors, but, to a large extent, our relationship behaviors can be observed through the lens of our Venus.

Venus represents our love language, indicating what we value and appreciate in relationships.

Additionally, Venus plays a significant role in shaping our behavior in relationships, as our actions often align with our values. In this series, you can explore different zodiac signs. For example, Mars represents how your sweetheart engages in conflict. And Mercury illustrates their communication style—(maybe a bit too chatty? Side-eye to you, Gemini), but Venus tends to take the lead in decoding romantic behaviors.

Life with an Aries

They're the best. At everything. Earth doesn't spin without them. As long as you don't let them know it actually does, you'll be fine.

Sex. Constant sex.

Tantrums. They're basically an angry five-year-old in an adult body. Give them ice cream and a hug and watch for flying objects.

They're the alpha. But if you don't challenge them, they're bored. But if they lose, tantrum. Tread carefully.

Life with a Taurus

Most of their time awake is spent eating food, planning what to eat, looking for new recipes, bookmarking new restaurants, asking where all the snacks are.

Rest of the time is spent sleeping, napping, complaining about the lack of a nap.

It's really simple: The answer to most of your questions is no.

Highly reliable, although you do have to understand that Taurus has its own definition of time. Roughly, 1 hour in normal people time = 6 hours in Taurus time.

Life with a Gemini

They often sound crazy and talk without interruption or punctuation and say random stuff like MAKE CHEESE GRATE AGAIN and it's mostly because there are so many thoughts added to each other but to be honest no one really understands Gemini even Gemini themselves.

Better if you can laugh at yourself because you're in for daily roasts.

Truth is really relative and depends on technicalities. If you want the right answer, ask the right question.

Pranks.

Life with a Cancer

If you think that solving conflict is as easy as just talking about it, boy are you wrong. Instead, expect subtle cues, frowning, and days of brooding to ultimately explode in a storm of screams and tears.

Family first. You're either in or out. Are you one of them or public enemy #1?

Food, cuddles, sex, babies, repeat.

Will viciously fight for you and protect you against "attacks" like a mama bear with her cub.

Life with a Leo

Don't you DARE give your attention to anyone else for more than a few seconds, or like a peacock they'll spread their feathers and that gets messy, trust me.

It's their way. There is no highway. Just their way.

You won't be bored. Sure as hell you're partying with Libra and Sagittarius keeping the economy up, thank you.

It's basically like getting a puppy. Lots of hair and belly rubs.

Life with a Virgo

Virgo is in the business of fixing things, and by marrying you, you just became their greatest project! Are you ready for your update?

Love is in the details. Don't expect grand romantic gestures but small daily things, like tolerating your toothbrush next to theirs.

Prude in the streets ... freak in the sheets!

You're about to understand what overthinking and overplanning means: Get ready for your breathing schedule!

Life with a Libra

Fairness inspector reporting for duty: Be prepared to be questioned, judged, and sentenced should you be found guilty.

Libras feel with their eyes and love with their brain. Act accordingly.

They'd like to do EVERYTHING with you and ideally you'd want to do EVERYTHING with them, unless they decided otherwise. In which case please give them their space.

Don't ever under-estimate the power of a Libra guilt trip. It's a game with no rules.

Life with a Scorpio

Doesn't really listen to what you say but thoroughly reads your body language to analyze "what you truly mean."

Complete devotion but also never too far away from plotting your murder.

Half invincible, half constantly butthurt, and in both cases just remains silent and stares. Tread carefully.

Still mad about that thing from 2 years ago.

Life with a Sagittarius

Life is an endless joke and nothing is ever serious.

If what you have to say is longer than 15 seconds, they stopped listening.

Absolutely zero filter, words come directly from the brain, blurted out through the mouth. Also, lots of swearing.

Makes to-do lists for everything. Starts most things on to-do list. Finishes none.

Life with a Capricorn

You spend TOO MUCH. No matter how much. It's TOO MUCH.

As reliable as the sun rising every morning.

Don't expect grand displays of emotions but they'll pick you up at the airport.

Loves to use work and responsibilities as a way of avoiding having to deal with you.

Life with an Aquarius

Partnering with Aquarius is like catching a rare Pokémon: We know they're almost impossible to find.

They're right, you're wrong. Just accept it and move on. It's easier for everyone involved.

They disappear. But don't worry, let them wander; they usually come back.

Anything is a restriction of freedom. Asking them to empty the dishwasher? They will do it WHEN THEY WANT, HOW THEY WANT, OK?

Life with a Pisces

There's going to be a lot of sleep and Netflix involved ... so hopefully you like being horizontal.

Arguing with a Pisces is like trying to catch the wind with your hand. Just lose yourself in their puppy eyes and let it go. It's never their fault.

Professional escapists.

Wouldn't hurt a fly. Would probably hold a little funeral for the fly that tragically died by hitting the garden window and write a poem about their grief.

Conclusion

As we conclude this journey through the zodiac signs and their myriad expressions in everyday life, leisure, and love, I hope you've enjoyed seeing how astrology offers us a lens through which to perceive and understand the complexities of human behavior.

I believe astrology is a language that transcends boundaries, offering us a common ground to connect and understand one another better, and I hope I have inspired in you the desire to learn more and discover yourself and others more deeply, through the language of the stars.

Thank you for joining me on this adventure. Until we meet again under the cosmic sky, keep shining bright and embracing the beautiful complexities that make you uniquely you.

Acknowledgments

Thank you to my mother for introducing me to astrology and teaching me that it's okay to be myself, however eccentric that might be. You were the first witch in the family, and I'm grateful to be carrying on your legacy. Thank you for allowing me to be whoever I want to be, free of expectations, and for teaching me, "Who cares what they think?"

Thank you to both of my parents for teaching me to be a freethinker and for giving me confidence by always trusting me and my instincts. You never expected me to be anything other than myself, and this led me to astrology.

To my devoted followers and clients: Thank you for filling my heart with joy and for helping me live my passion while staying true to myself.

And finally, thank you to my agent, Laura Mazer, for giving me the opportunity I always dreamed of, and thank you to my editor, Rachel Hiles, and the team at Chronicle Books for making this book come (beautifully) true while honoring my vision.